The Baptismal Liturgy

E. C. Whitaker

Vicar of Plumpton Wall
Honorary Canon of Carlisle

D1259044

LONDON
SPCK

First published by the Faith Press in 1965
Second edition 1981
SPCK
Holy Trinity Church
Marylebone Road
London NW1 4DU

©E. C. Whitaker 1965, 1981

Typeset by Pioneer
Printed in Great Britain by
Ebenezer Baylis & Son Ltd
The Trinity Press,
Worcester, and London

ISBN 0 281 03809 0

Contents

Author's Foreword

The first edition of this book was published by the Faith Press in 1965 and is now out of print. The sub-title was *An Introduction to Baptism in the Western Church.* In this second edition some attention has been paid to the eastern rites in their early stages and the first two chapters have been completely rewritten. Two chapters have been added, one on the new initiation rites of the Church of England and one on those of the Roman Catholic Church. The chapter on bibliography has been brought up to date.

It is not possible to study the history of the rite without constant reference to the actual text at various stages of its development. It was for this reason that in 1960 I translated and edited a number of such texts which were published under the title *Documents of the Baptismal Liturgy.* A second and revised edition of that work was published by SPCK in 1970, and it is to that second edition that the references are made in the present book.

E. C. WHITAKER

1

The Foundations of the Liturgy

1 THE BAPTISMAL WASHING

Today when we use the word 'baptize' we refer to a ritual occasion with religious significance which takes place most probably in a church building. It involves a candidate, infant or adult, an officiant, parents, godparents or sponsors, and possibly a wider congregation, all with their appropriate parts to play. Words are said and actions performed. The word 'baptize' today may conjure up in our minds the totality of such a familiar occasion. But in origin it is a Greek word and its original meaning had no religious significance. It meant simply 'immerse' or 'drown'. It could be used of a ship sinking or a man drowning or being drowned: and a man 'baptized' in wine meant a man who was soaked in wine, or drunk. The idea of perishing was never far away. When we encounter the word in the New Testament it is not always clear whether it is used in the developed, technical sense to refer to a ritual occasion or in the primary and secular sense of immersion. In many cases it is possible that both senses of the word are present in the writer's mind.[1]

The New Testament provides no certain evidence that baptism in the apostolic age was performed by immersion. Alan Richardson has indeed stated positively[2] that immersion was the regular practice and justifies this by quoting Hebrews 10.22 (our guilty hearts sprinkled clean, our bodies washed with pure water), but it is doubtful whether this text justifies a confident conclusion. Nevertheless the primary meaning of 'baptize' suggests that immersion, whether total or less than total, may well have been customary, and the New Testament teaching that in baptism we are united with Christ in his death is better symbolized by immersion than by a simple act of pouring a little water or sprinkling it. In the baptism of infants today it is noticeable that the pouring of a little water on the child's forehead is not a very eloquent symbol of dying with Christ. Another consideration which might lead us to think that Christian baptism was originally by immersion is that in the baptism of proselytes the Jews regarded it as a matter of some importance that the candidate passed wholly beneath the water. But the force of this argument is diminished by the uncertainty about the date when the Jews adopted the practice of proselyte baptism and whether they did so before the apostolic age.[3]

In later centuries we have occasional indications that the Church baptized by total immersion. Certainly this seems to be indicated in the *catecheses* of Theodore of Mopsuestia and of Narsai (DBL, pp. 49, 55),[4] and strongly suggested in many accounts in the Syrian apocryphal works of baptisms in the sea, in lakes, and in man-made tanks. The *Apostolic Tradition* of Hippolytus seems to regard immersion as the preferable practice (DBL, p. 5). But the evidence of many fonts and baptisteries erected for the baptism of adults from the beginning of the third century, both in east and west, is sufficient to demonstrate that, when baptism was administered away from natural deep water, total immersion was the exception rather than the rule.[5] With rare exceptions, the baptismal tanks were simply not big enough for total immersion. The evidence provided by the dimensions of baptisteries is supported by the paintings in the catacombs and elsewhere which show men standing up to the knees or the waist while water is poured over their head from a bowl or directed over them from a water course flowing into the tank. This may fairly be called immersion, although it is not total immersion. The rubrics of the Sarum rite (DBL, p. 247), followed by the Prayer Book of 1549, direct that the child shall be dipped once with his face to the north, once with his face to the south, and once face downwards in the water. This custom may well have been very ancient, since it seems to be indicated in the Gelasian Sacramentary (DBL, p. 188), and it explains the size of many medieval fonts.

The alternatives to immersion are either the affusion (pouring) of water or aspersion (the sprinkling of water), and one or the other has been accepted in the place of immersion from very early times. Thus the *Didache* (DBL, p. 1) allows affusion if the water available is not sufficient for immersion. St Cyprian attests aspersion as the method employed when people were baptized on the sick bed; and although clinical baptism had a bad name in the early Church this was only because the sincerity of adults baptized in such circumstances was open to question, and not because of any theological deficiency in baptism by affusion or aspersion. In the Middle Ages the Council of Chelsea (816) recorded a preference for immersion on the imagined ground that 'our Lord was immersed three times in the waves of Jordan', and Aquinas thought immersion better because it was more commonly practised: but in each case the preference which is displayed for immersion implies the recognition that affusion or aspersion was also acceptable. The Book of Common Prayer therefore follows a very ancient tradition when it shows a preference for dipping, or immersion, and only allows affusion 'if they certify the child is weak'. In such circumstances the Prayer Book requires the pouring, or affusion, of water, but the difference between affusion and aspersion seems very slight. It is worth noting that aspersion is attested by Cyprian and later in the Stowe Missal (DBL, pp. 2, 220), if we are justified in supposing that the Latin word *spargere* implies aspersion. Such notable 17th and 18th century writers as Bishop Sparrow, Jeremy Taylor, Hamon L'Estrange, and Charles Wheatly write of pouring and sprinkling as though they were the same thing: and the Prayer Book catechism as it stood between 1604 and 1662 spoke of dipping and sprinkling as alternative methods in baptism.

From an early date the practice of using three immersions in baptism seems to have been almost universal. St Paul explained baptism as a kind of *mimesis* of the death and resurrection of Christ, and by a natural extension of this teaching the three washings were sometimes explained as analogous to our Lord's three days in the tomb. This very possibly explains the origin of the triple washing in baptism, but its widespread use is most probably best explained by the Trinitarian character of the Christian faith and the Trinitarian formularies which were universally adopted in baptism. The three washings corresponded to the invocation of each of the three Persons of the Trinity. Exceptions to this are rare. The fourth century Arians known as Eunomians practised only one immersion. In Spain (DBL, pp. 115, 224, 226) there was a dispute between those who held that triple washing favoured the Arian teaching which recognized three Gods in the Trinity and therefore used only one, and others who claimed that single washing implied the Sabellian teaching that in the one Godhead there is no distinction between the three Persons. The Bible has nothing to say on the subject and no more has the Prayer Book. Theologically speaking it does not matter whether there is one washing or three, or more. But since the Church baptizes into the threefold name of God, it has usually seemed natural to use a threefold washing.

Tertullian is our earliest witness (DBL, p. 7; see also pp. 4, 11) for the blessing of water at baptism, and the later liturgical books provide elaborate prayers (DBL, pp. 119, 138, 160, 186) and ceremony for the purpose. It is possible that the impulse which first led the Church to use such prayers was the change from the original situation in which baptisms necessarily took place in rivers and lakes where the water was moving and alive to the more developed situation when tanks or fonts were constructed for the purpose.[6] The evidence is plain that from the time of Tertullian the blessing of water was believed to invest it with power to effect the purposes of baptism which it did not otherwise possess. But the real value of the prayer as it developed was that it became a vehicle to set out the theology of baptism and in particular the associations which establish water as the appropriate matter of the sacrament. The prayers descanted on the symbolism of water in all its rich variety, and drew largely on the Old Testament for their imagery. They

4

drew on the story of creation, where water is associated with the Holy Spirit; on the rivers which flowed from Eden to refresh the whole earth; on the Flood, where water had the two-fold effect of cleansing the world from wickedness and giving a new beginning to virtue; on the Exodus, where the water was a cause both of life and death; on the water which flowed from the rock in the wilderness to be a source of life. By such means the prayers explained the power of water in Christian baptism to convey the refreshment of the Holy Spirit, cleansing from sin, death to past evil, and resurrection to new life. But these benefits do not proceed from the water itself, but from the Passion and Resurrection of our Lord. This is why the prayers often identify the water of baptism with the water which was shed with his blood from the side of Christ, and why the administration of baptism came to be associated with Easter.

2   THE FORM OF BAPTISM

Baptism does not consist only in a washing in water, however administered: the form of words which accompanies the washing is an equally necessary part of the sacrament. This was expressed in a famous passage of St Augustine in his *Discourses on St John's Gospel.* Commenting on the text, 'Now you are clean because of the word which I have spoken to you' (John 15.3), Augustine said:

> Why does he not say 'You are clean because of the baptism with which you have been washed', but 'because of the word which I have spoken to you', unless the reason is that even in the water it is the word which cleanses? Take away the word and what is the water but (plain) water? But when the word comes into association with the material element, a sacrament comes into being, as though the word itself took visible form. For when the Lord washed the disciples' feet he had said, 'A man who has bathed needs only to wash his feet and he is altogether clean' (John 13.10). Whence does the water acquire such power that by touching the body it is able to

5

cleanse the heart, if it is not through the action of the word: and not because the word is spoken but because it is believed? . . . Read the Apostle and see what he adds: 'cleansing it (i.e. the Church) with the washing of water in the word, so that he might sanctify it' (Eph. 5.26). This cleansing therefore is not to be attributed to a fluid and unstable element, unless we add 'in the word'. This word of faith works with such efficacy in the Church of God that . . . it can cleanse even a tiny child, although it is not yet able to believe with the heart unto righteousness or confess with the mouth unto salvation.[7]

So baptism requires the material element of water in association with 'the word'. This teaching is reflected in the Prayer Book catechism, which tells us that the outward and visible sign in baptism is 'water wherein the person is baptized in the name of the Father and of the Son and of the Holy Ghost'. The baptismal liturgy has grown up round the performance of a washing with water accompanied by an invocation of the Holy Trinity, which in the language of medieval theology are known as the matter and the form of baptism. Nothing else, not even the sign of the cross, is necessary: these two things are essential, and form the core of every baptismal liturgy in Christendom.

An early hint of a form of words employed in Christian baptism is found in the passage in the Acts of the Apostles which reads: 'For as yet he was fallen upon none of them, only they were baptized in the name of the Lord Jesus' (Acts 8.16; see also Acts 19.15; Rom. 6.3). This may mean to say no more than that what they had received was Christian baptism and not the baptism of John or of the Jews, but it certainly suggests that a more or less precise formula may have been in use which included the words 'in the name of Jesus'. This possibility is supported by the instruction in the *Didache* (DBL, p. 1) which says 'Let no-one eat or drink of your eucharist but such as have been baptized in the name of the Lord', and even more by a passage in the apocryphal *Acts of Paul,*[8] according to which Thecla 'cast herself into the water in the name of Jesus Christ, saying "I baptize myself in the name of Jesus Christ unto the last day".' The evidence therefore suggests that a form of baptism 'in the name of Jesus' may have been used in apostolic times and may have continued well into the second century.

According to St Matthew's Gospel, our Lord commanded the apostles to 'teach all nations, baptizing them in the name of the Father and of the Son and of the Holy Spirit' (Matt. 28.19). On the face of it this seems to suggest that from the beginning Jesus had enjoined and the apostles had used the same form of words which is familiar to us in baptism today, that is to say, *I baptize you in the name of the Father and of the Son and of the Holy Spirit.* But there are difficulties about this. We may think it out of character that our Lord should give such precise instructions about liturgical details. We may also think it strange that he should speak of himself in detached terms as one of the Persons of the Trinity. And finally, the passage in St Matthew's Gospel seems to be inconsistent with those other passages in the New Testament which speak of baptism 'in the name of Jesus'. All these difficulties may be resolved if we accept the view that the author of the first Gospel was not attempting to quote our Lord's exact words but that he was reflecting the liturgical practice to which he was himself accustomed. It is widely believed that St Matthew's Gospel was written in Syria, and there is no lack of evidence that the same formula which the Gospel suggests was used in Syria, with minor variations, from an early date. The *Didache* is the earliest witness with the words 'Baptize in the name of the Father . . .'. *The Acts of Xanthippe and Polyxena* (DBL, p. 19) represent St Paul baptizing with the words, 'We baptize you in the name . . .'. And in the *History of John the Son of Zebedee* (DBL, p. 21) St John uses the words, 'In the name of the Father; in the name of the Son; in the name of the Spirit of Holiness'. It seems likely therefore that the earliest forms of the baptismal formula which were used in Syria often began, 'I baptize you in the name . . .' or 'We baptize you in the name . . .'. However we learn from St John Chrysostom and others (DBL, pp. 36, 41, 55)[9] that late in the fourth century the Syrian Church abandoned this form and substituted the form, 'N. is baptized in the name . . .', which has characterized the baptismal liturgy of the Churches of the east ever since. According to Chrysostom the reasons for adopting this passive, impersonal form, were first to indicate that the bestowal of the sacrament is an act of the Holy Trinity rather than of the minister, and therefore secondly that any unworthiness on the part of the minister does not hinder the efficacy of the sacrament.

It is customary to speak of the form 'I baptize you . . .' as the western form of baptism and 'N. is baptized . . .' as the eastern form; and it is certainly true that the Churches of East and West today observe this difference in their practice and have done so for many centuries. Originally however, and for a considerable time, both of these forms were confined to the eastern, Syrian, Church. Outside Syria, at Rome and Alexandria and throughout the West, the Trinitarian character of Christian baptism was declared in quite a different way. The earliest example appears in the *Apostolic Tradition* (DBL, p. 5) of Hippolytus, *c.* 215. According to this the candidate for baptism stood in the water and was asked 'Do you believe in God the Father Almighty?'. He answered 'I believe' and was dipped once in the water. The next question ran, 'Do you believe in Jesus Christ, who was born of the Holy Spirit and the Virgin Mary . . . and will come to judge the living and the dead?'. Again the candidate answered 'I believe', and was dipped the second time. Thirdly he was asked 'Do you believe in the Holy Spirit in the Holy Church?', and for the third time he assented and was dipped. No other words were spoken, and none were necessary. The three questions and answers themselves constituted the form of the sacrament, for when the candidate had assented to the three questions upon the Holy Trinity he had indeed been baptized in the name of the Father and the Son and the Holy Spirit.

We have already noted a passage in St Augustine's *Discourses on St John's Gospel* in which he draws attention to the importance of the 'word' in baptism. If we ask what exact 'word'

St Augustine had in mind and what liturgical practice provided the background of his argument, we may suspect that it was not different from that attested by Hippolytus. Augustine says that the word is effective 'not because it is spoken but because it is believed', and he describes it as 'the word of faith'. Language of this kind suggests that the efficacious word in baptism to which Augustine referred was not the formula which we use today but the triple interrogation on the faith. The same conclusion is suggested by the correspondence between the deacon Ferrandus of Carthage and bishop Fulgentius of Ruspe (DBL, p. 108) in Africa. Ferrandus was concerned about a candidate who was brought, mute and paralysed, to baptism and had since died. He had not been able to answer the customary interrogations, and the problem therefore was to know whether his 'lack of speech had damaged his hope of blessedness'. If the form 'I baptize you in the name . . .' had been in use, this question could not have arisen. As it was, the bishop's reply was that the candidate had virtually answered the questions in the course of his preparation, and therefore that he had indeed been saved in baptism.

It is clear from the works of Tertullian (DBL, pp. 9f) and St Ambrose (DBL, pp. 129f) that the form of baptism which is attested by Hippolytus was used also in Africa and Milan. The *Gelasian Sacramentary* (DBL, pp. 188, 195) witnesses that the practice at Rome in the early sixth century was not essentially different, and the Stowe Missal (DBL, p. 220) shows that it survived in Ireland as late as the year 800. But already in the early fourth century the process had begun by which the simpler form of baptism which prevailed in Syria was to make its way through the western Church until it finally displaced the triple interrogations and their answers from their position as the accepted form of baptism. The process appears to begin in Egypt, for the Syrian form is first attested outside Syria in the Egyptian recension of the *Apostolic Tradition* known as the *Canons of Hippolytus* (DBL, p. 90), written about the year 336. There are passages in St Augustine's treatise *De Baptismo contra Donatistas* (DBL, pp. 105f) which suggest that it may

9

possibly have been known to St Augustine, that is to say, that it may have been adopted in Hippo before the year 430. For Spain it is attested by Hildephonsus (DBL, p. 115) of Toledo, *c.*650, and its earliest attestation for the Gallican Church is in the Gallican Missals (DBL, pp. 162, 212) which date from about 700. Finally there is clear evidence that it was used in Rome[10] by the year 726, and from this point it has come to be accepted as the customary form of baptism in the western Church as it had been in the eastern Church from the beginning. The fact that today the western form is the active 'I baptize you. . .' while the eastern Church has 'N. is baptized . . .' arises most probably from the accident that the process by which the Syrian form spread into the West began, as we have seen, about the year 336, that is to say, before the eastern Church had resolved on the change from the active to the passive form.

The origin of the interrogation on the faith can probably be traced to apostolic times. Thus in the Acts of the Apostles, at the baptism by Philip of the Ethiopian eunuch, Philip said 'If you believe with all your heart, you may', and the eunuch replied 'I believe that Jesus is the Son of God' (Acts 8.37). It is most probable that this verse does not belong to the original text of the Acts, but it is certainly a very early addition and records primitive practice. It is very likely that St Paul had a similar dialogue in mind when he said of Timothy that he had 'professed a good profession before many witnesses' (1 Tim. 6.12), and St Peter when he spoke of 'the answer of a good conscience' (1 Peter 3.21).

The questions on the faith are the source from which the Apostles' Creed originated. They served to emphasize the importance of faith in the baptized person, and make it clear that he is one who above all puts his faith in the Holy Trinity. They explain why St Augustine called baptism 'the sacrament of faith'. When these questions and their answers were ultimately replaced in the western Church by the now familiar form which had been introduced from Syria, they did not disappear from the rite. They held their place immediately before the baptismal washing, and so continued to bear witness to the central importance of faith in the baptized person.

3 POST-BAPTISMAL CEREMONIES

Throughout the history of the western Church baptism has invariably been followed by certain other ceremonies which are known today as 'confirmation'. The earliest sure evidence for these ceremonies is to be found in Tertullian's treatise *Concerning Baptism,* written in the year 198, and in the *Apostolic Tradition, c.*215. According to the *Apostolic Tradition,* when the candidates had dried themselves after baptism and resumed their clothes, the bishop prayed that they might be filled with the Holy Spirit (or that they might be worthy to be filled with the Holy Spirit), and went on to anoint them, and sign them with the cross; and Tertullian attests a similar performance. After this the Eucharist was celebrated and the newly baptized received communion for the first time. Thus baptism, the post-baptismal ceremonies, and the Eucharist formed one complete liturgical occasion. It is important to note that children and infants were baptized with their parents, received the anointing and laying on of the hand after baptism, and then with their parents received Holy Communion.

It is not likely that an occasion such as this, and the lengthy and ceremonious course of preparation which preceded it, could have taken place very often. The *Apostolic Tradition* does not say that it took place only at Easter, but Tertullian evidently regarded Easter as the most suitable season, 'for then was accomplished our Lord's Passion, and in it we are baptized'. In any case it was not long after this date that baptism came to be normally restricted to the Paschal season, and the development of Lent was related to the preparation of the candidates. To this day the blessing of the font and the baptism of candidates continue to characterize the celebration of the Easter vigil.

The unity of the rites of initiation as it is attested by Tertullian and the *Apostolic Tradition* and other western sources (DBL,

11

pp. 127f, 151f, 184f) in the following centuries was eventually broken: baptism at Easter came to be the exception rather than the rule, and baptism came to be separated from the rites which followed it. From an early date this development was implicit in the practice of clinical baptism, since in the nature of the circumstances this had to be available at all times and might have to be performed at times when the bishop was not at hand to administer the post-baptismal rites. But the effective reasons for disintegration were first the doctrine of St Augustine that infants (and others) who die unbaptized are eternally damned, and secondly the insistence of the Roman Church that the post-baptismal ceremonies were the sole prerogative of the bishop. The effect of St Augustine's doctrine was that, in days when the infant mortality rate was very high, parents were anxious to secure baptism for their children without waiting for the following Easter; and the clergy was ready to comply with their wishes. The consequence was that baptism came to be administered at many times during the year (DBL, pp. 225, 228), and finally on any Sunday. In Spain and the Gallican Churches (DBL, pp. 121, 162, 212, 220) the post-baptismal anointing was then performed by the priest at baptism, and thus baptism and the rites which followed it were not separated. But in the end the Roman practice prevailed which restricted confirmation to the bishop (and the firm line taken by the Roman Church at this point is exemplified by the letter of Pope Innocent to the Gallican bishop Decentius (DBL, p. 229). Since bishops could not be present at every baptism it was inevitable that baptism became separated from the ceremonies which followed it. However, once children were baptized it was not always apparent to their parents that there was any need to bring them to the bishop for the remaining ceremonies. Nor was it always easy or possible to do so. Bishops therefore, through their synods and councils, began to insist on the importance of bringing children to confirmation: and to make this possible the age for confirmation was variously determined at ages from seven to eleven years old.[11] With confirmation thus deferred to this age, it was a sensible development when the instruction of children in such basic elements of faith as the Creed, the Lord's Prayer, and the *Ave Maria* came to be associated with it. This practice was crystallized in the order of confirmation of the second English Prayer Book of 1552, when the laying on of hands was linked with the recitation of the catechism, which the rubrics interpret as a renewal of baptismal vows. From the pastoral point of view this was a wise development, but the reformers went too far when they affirmed that the renewal of baptismal vows was a normal practice of the primitive Church.[12] There is not a shred of evidence to support this.

The Church of England does not recognize confirmation as a 'sacrament of the gospel', and accordingly its official formularies do not define any outward signs of form or matter for its administration. Historically the actions by which confirmation has been administered and the prayers and other forms which accompany the actions have varied considerably. In the *Apostolic Tradition* the actions included the imposition of the bishop's hand, anointing, and the sign of the cross, and it is also possible that the bishop extended his hands over the candidates while he said a prayer for the Holy Spirit. As the rites developed we find that the anointing and the imposition of the hand were the principal features of the rite, but they do not always appear in the same order. In the Roman rite, which came to prevail throughout the West, we find that the imposition of the hand disappeared altogether, so that only the anointing remained in the Sarum rite on the eve of the Reformation (DBL, p. 252). The reformers altered this, abandoning anointing and replacing it with the imposition of the hand, because they regarded one as scriptural but not the other. The forms of words which accompanied the actions were as varied as the actions themselves. There is however one prayer which stands out from the rest both for its antiquity and for its widespread currency. This is the prayer for the sevenfold gifts of the Spirit which is still preserved in the Prayer Book and in the forms of confirmation service in the Alternative Service Book. This prayer, which is based on a passage in Isaiah (11.2), is first attested in the correspondence of Pope Siricius and quoted soon after in the treatise *Concerning the Sacraments* (DBL, pp. 131, 133), written by St Ambrose about 390. It is possible that it is a developed form of the prayer in the *Apostolic Tradition,* 'O Lord God, who didst count these worthy . . .'. In the *Apostolic Tradition* the bishop is to lay his hand on the candidates as he says this prayer; and in the *Gelasian Sacramentary* (DBL, p. 188) he is likewise to lay his hand on the candidates as he says the prayer for the sevenfold gifts of the Spirit. It does not seem likely that he repeated this prayer in its entirety over each of perhaps a hundred candidates as he laid his hand on the head of each: it is more probable that he extended his hands over them all while he said the prayer once. This is possibly what Tertullian had in mind when he wrote 'flesh is overshadowed (*adumbratur*) by the imposition of the hand': and later Roman forms of the service specify that the bishop is to extend his hands over the candidate as he said this prayer.[13]

The purpose and meaning of the post-baptismal ceremonies is a matter of controversy.[14] On the one hand some scholars have claimed that they constitute a sacrament possessing its own efficacy: they understand it either as a separate sacrament distinct from baptism or as an essential part of baptism itself and related to it as closely as the cup is to the bread in the sacrament of the Eucharist. The purpose of the sacrament is to convey the gift of the Holy Spirit. Some have not hesitated to carry this belief to its logical conclusion and claim that baptism without confirmation is incomplete, that the person who has been baptized but not confirmed has not received the gift of the Spirit and is only half a Christian. On the other hand there are those who claim that confirmation is a mere ceremony which achieves nothing of itself. They would understand it as a simple blessing accompanied by prayer that the candidate might grow in the Spirit, possessing no more efficacy than we should attach to any other prayer; or as a ceremony designed to unfold the content of baptism and illuminate the truth that the Spirit has already been given in the waters of baptism. These two approaches to confirmation are reflected in the central petition of the prayer for the sevenfold gifts of the Spirit, for historically this prayer has taken two forms. In the *Gelasian Sacramentary* the prayer was, 'Send upon them thy Holy Spirit', and the Sarum rite and the first English Prayer Book of 1549 were not essentially different; but in the second English Prayer Book of 1552 this was altered to read, 'Strengthen them with the Holy Ghost and daily increase in them thy manifold gifts of grace', and this has remained unaltered in the Prayer Book of 1662. Of these two forms the first reflects the view that confirmation is an occasion for the gift of the Spirit, while the second suggests that confirmation is an occasion to pray for an increase in the gifts of the Spirit whom we have already received.

There is a third interpretation of confirmation, which however we may safely dismiss. This would affirm that baptism conveys such gifts as are appropriate to infancy, while confirmation conveys gifts which are appropriate to maturity. This may have seemed reasonable in an age when virtually all candidates for baptism were infants and confirmation was normally deferred to later years. But it takes no account of the ⟨or baptism to adults!⟩ historical fact that confirmation was for a long time given to infants. No explanation of confirmation can therefore be satisfactory which is not applicable to infant confirmation. The attempt to explain confirmation as a 'sacrament of growth' or as the 'ordination of the laity' does not meet with the facts of history.

The origin of confirmation is as much debated as its meaning. There are a number of passages in the New Testament which have been taken to indicate a two-part rite of initiation. Thus St Peter's command, 'Be baptized . . . and you will receive the gift of the Holy Spirit' (Acts 2.38), has been taken to imply that baptism was from the first followed by a second rite to convey the gift of the Spirit. Similarly the accounts of our Lord's baptism have been taken to follow a dual pattern by which our

15

Lord was first baptized and only after that did the Holy Spirit descend on him. A dual pattern has also been noted in the fact that our Lord imparted the Spirit to the disciples on two occasions, first on the day of his resurrection (John 20.22), and later on the day of Pentecost. Some passages in St Paul's epistles have been held to imply a two-stage rite of initiation, for example, 'He saved us through the water of rebirth and the renewing power of the Holy Spirit' (Titus 3.5). Evidence for the practice of anointing in apostolic times has been found in the First Epistle of St John, 'But you have been anointed by the Holy One' (1 John 2.20, 27; see also 2 Cor. 1.22). Evidence for the laying on of hands seems to be provided by the occasion when Peter and John came from Jerusalem to lay hands on the Samaritan converts, with the result that they received the Holy Spirit (Acts 8.15-17; see also 19.5,6). The reference in the Epistle to the Hebrews to the laying on of hands (Heb. 6.2) has also suggested that confirmation by the imposition of the hand was practised in the apostolic Church.

It is uncertain whether any of these passages or the sum of them is sufficient to demonstrate that baptism in the apostolic age was customarily followed by a second sacramental act for the gift of the Holy Spirit. Passages which link baptism and the gift of the Spirit may indicate that the gift of the Spirit belongs to baptism itself. The accounts of our Lord's baptism do not necessarily indicate a two-stage event, and the eastern Church certainly regarded the baptism and the descent of the Spirit as one event. References to anointing may just as well be understood in a metaphorical as a material sense, as it must be in St Peter's affirmation that God 'anointed' Jesus with the Holy Spirit (Acts 10.38). The references in the Acts to the laying on of hands may fairly be understood[15] as accounts of exceptional occasions rather than of the customary procedure. The most which we can safely conclude from the New Testament evidence is that the apostles may sometimes have laid hands on the newly baptized, but not invariably and not of necessity. Between the last book of the New Testament to be written and the first certain testimony to post-baptismal ceremonies in Tertullian's treatise *Concerning Baptism* there is an interval of a hundred years or more, during which liturgical developments may have taken place. It is possible that the practice of anointing may have developed from the custom of the ancient world to take oil to the bath where today we take soap and other toiletries. Another possibility is that both anointing and the imposition of the hand were introduced into Christian practice from the initiation rites of the semi-Christian gnostic sects.

4 CONFIRMATION IN THE EASTERN CHURCH?

It is well known that at the present day the post-baptismal ceremonies of the eastern Church are not fundamentally different from those of the West. After baptism the candidate is anointed, and this anointing is understood to convey the gift of the Holy Spirit. The anointing is performed by the priest at baptism, and it is given to infants no less than to adults. The importance of the study of the eastern rite is that it shows that originally there was no such ceremony after the baptismal washing: the candidate went from baptism to take his place at the Eucharist with no ceremonies between the two. A rite consisting of an anointing before baptism, the baptism itself, and then the Eucharist without any post-baptismal ceremonies is attested in many early Syrian sources. The earliest witness[16] to a rite of this kind is the *Testament of Levi* (190-225), where the following passage is recognized to be a description of the initiation rite: 'The first anointed me with holy oil . . . the second washed me with pure water and fed me with bread and wine'. Similarly the *Acts of Xanthippe and Polyxena* (c.250) (DBL, pp. 19f) describe initiation as 'the invocation of a new name and the unction of oil and the laver of water', and the same document shows that the 'laver of water' was followed immediately by the Eucharist. A rite of this kind is well exemplified in the *Didascalia,* where the priest anoints the forehead and the rest of the body is then anointed by some other person, and in the baptismal instructions of St John Chrysostom, where the two parts of the anointing are separated by an interval of twenty-four hours: and in many other sources (DBL, pp. 12, 31ff; see also 13f, 21f, 50f). At first sight therefore the early rite of the eastern Church had nothing to correspond either with 'confirmation' as it was practised in the West or with the New Testament evidence, such as it is, for a two-stage rite of initiation in which baptism was followed by a second rite for the gift of the Spirit. But if a rite is not practised universally, it is not likely to be essential. In order to escape from the unwelcome conclusion that the eastern Church had originally no separate rite for the gift of the Spirit, distinct from baptism, some scholars[17] have drawn attention to the fact that Syrian writers frequently refer to the imposition of the hand in baptism, and it is true that St John Chrysostom seems to associate this action, among others, with the imparting of the Holy Spirit. But St John is exceptional in this respect, and the imposition of the hand at the moment of baptism is not more than the action which was required by the practical necessity of baptizing, as may be seen for instance in the *Apostolic Tradition*. Other scholars have drawn attention to the anointing before baptism, and claimed that this is the sacramental action by which the gift of the Holy Spirit was bestowed. Again, it is true that a number of Syrian writers interpret the pre-baptismal anointing in this way, but it is equally true that others do not. St John Chrysostom, for instance, interprets it quite differently. And while sources such as the Epiphany Hymns of St Ephrem suggest that the Spirit is bestowed in the anointing before baptism, the same sources suggest also, in other passages, that the Spirit is bestowed in baptism itself. J. D. C. Fisher has shown that Syrian sources refer the gift of the Spirit in Christian initiation variously to the pre-baptismal anointing, to the water of baptism, to the imposition of the hand in the moment of baptism, and to the Eucharist which followed baptism: some of them associate the gift with more than one of these elements in the rite. But Fisher stops short of the conclusion to which his evidence and his argument point, that the Syrian Church had no clear doctrine that any one sacramental act was essential for the imparting of the Holy Spirit, unless it was the act of baptism itself. Dom Bernard Botte's conclusion[18] is that 'the pre-baptismal anointing signified the intention of conferring, at the same time as the baptism, the gift of the Spirit. It is not a separate rite, rather the two effects are produced conjointly by the same rite. Unless we suppose that they intended to confer the gift of the Spirit before the baptism — which seems absurd to me and is excluded by St John Chrysostom — I do not see any other explanation for this practice.'

5   THE RENUNCIATION

There is nothing in the New Testament which suggests that a formal act of renunciation of the devil was made before baptism in the apostolic age. In the western Church the earliest evidence for a renunciation is in the *Apostolic Tradition*. It appears there as a preliminary to baptism, and the candidate addresses the devil directly, saying 'I renounce thee, Satan, and all thy service, and all thy works'. Tertullian (DBL, pp. 9f; see also p. 107) seems to indicate that a renunciation might take place more than once, on one occasion as an immediate preliminary to baptism but also at some earlier point in the course of preparation. In the course of time the form of direct address to Satan was recast in the form of questions, 'Dost thou renounce the devil, etc?'. St Ambrose (DBL, pp. 128, 131) indicates that in Milan two questions were asked, and the later rites of Milan (DBL, pp. 137, 143, 148) preserve the same tradition. In Roman (DBL, p. 183) and Gallican sources, however, the renunciation takes the form of three questions. The renunciation is an act quite distinct from the profession of faith in baptism. Thus in the *Apostolic Tradition* the profession of faith takes place while the candidate stands in the water of baptism, but the renunciation is made before he enters the water; in the *Gelasian Sacramentary* the renunciation takes place during the Saturday morning assembly of the candidates and the profession of faith is part of the action of baptism; according to St Ambrose the renunciation was made before the font was approached, and in the later rites of Milan it was performed, as at Rome, on the Saturday morning before baptism. The renunciation thus belonged to the preliminaries while the questions on the faith belonged to the baptism itself. It was therefore not a sound development when the Gallican Church joined the questions of the renunciation and the questions on the faith into one series, (DBL, pp. 110, 114, 211, 215 (cf. 220), 246) but this development was preserved in the Sarum rite (but not in the Roman books of the same period), and consequently in the English Prayer Book from 1549 to 1662.

In the eastern Church the earliest testimony (DBL, pp. 28, 32) to the renunciation comes to us from St Cyril of Jerusalem and the *Apostolic Constitutions* in the middle of the fourth century. Evidence for earlier centuries however is scanty, and it is possible that the eastern Church had included a renunciation in its liturgical forms long before the earliest evidence for it. According to St Cyril the renunciation took place in 'the outer chamber', before the candidate entered the 'Holy of Holies' for baptism: and in the *Apostolic Constitutions* it comes before the blessing of the water. A noticeable feature of the renunciation as it was performed in the East is that it was invariably followed by an 'Act of Adherence', either to Christ or to the Holy Trinity, and the two acts are known as the *apotaxis* and *syntaxis*. Thus in St Cyril's account, after the renunciation the candidate went on to say, 'I believe in the Father and in the Son and in the Holy Ghost, and in one baptism of repentance'. Moreover the candidates were made to suit their actions to their words. To make the renunciation they faced west 'to the region of sensible darkness', and to make the act of adherence they turned to face east, that is to the light of Christ. The details both of the *apotaxis* and the *syntaxis* vary as they appear in different sources, (DBL, pp. 37, 39, 47, 50, 57, 58, 62, 70, 77, 89, 93f) but they always appear together as one liturgical construction among the preliminaries of the eastern rite, and thus distinguish the eastern rite from the western. The western rite never included a *syntaxis*: it had no need of it since a profession of faith was from the beginning closely interwoven with the triple washing of baptism. It is true that St Ambrose appears to hint at the practice of turning east towards Christ at baptism, and E. J. Yarnold has inferred[19] from this that he was also accustomed to the practice of turning west for the renunciation and east for a *syntaxis*. But this goes far beyond the evidence. There are other cases in St Ambrose's treatises where he borrows from eastern imagery to expound the services, but that is not to say that he followed the eastern order. And Dr Yarnold's contention that Tertullian also was acquainted with the *syntaxis* depends on a needlessly forced translation of the Latin.

2

Basic Patterns and their Development

We may think it improbable that Christians of the second and third generations, in places as far apart as Antioch and Rome, Alexandria and Carthage, would follow one identical order in the administration of baptism, or that they would have in front of them a written form which they felt obliged to follow. Certainly there is no evidence that this was the case. It seems more likely that so long as what was essential was duly performed, the manner of its performance and any peripheral additions would vary from place to place, and that in the early days of the Church's history there would be many varieties of custom, all with an equal claim to be apostolic. Nevertheless in the course of time rites tend to crystallize. They also tend to reflect the local culture in which they develop. If in the foregoing chapter we have sometimes classified our evidence as 'eastern' or 'western', this is because it comes from one or other of the two main cultural backgrounds in which the Church grew up. The western Church was surrounded by the Hellenistic culture of the Graeco-Roman world, where the language was first Greek and later Latin. This covered the greater part of the Mediterranean basin and included Alexandria and Egypt. The eastern (Syrian) rite is associated with Antioch and inland Edessa. The culture of Antioch was Greek, but the language of the indigenous population was Aramaic (Syriac) and their culture Semitic. The Syrian rite ultimately spread to Byzantium (Constantinople) and all the Churches of the eastern world. It is thus possible to distinguish from an early date two different patterns of initiation rite, one associated with the East and the other with the West. The difference between them emerges clearly if we summarize in tabular form the evidence which we have already examined.

THE EASTERN RITE

Renunciation
1 *apotaxis* (renunciation, facing west)
2 *syntaxis* (act of adherence, facing east)

Pre-baptismal anointing
1 by the minister to the forehead
2 by some other person to the whole body

Baptism   accompanied by the form 'I baptize you in the name . . .'

THE WESTERN RITE

Renunciation   without *syntaxis*

Baptism   accompanied by triple interrogation of the faith
(but no form 'I baptize you in the name . . .')

Post-baptismal ceremonies
prayer for the Holy Spirit
anointing of forehead
imposition of the hand

From this table we may see that the eastern and western rites were distinguished from each other by certain features which they did not hold in common. Peculiar to the East were the *syntaxis,* the two-part anointing before baptism, and the form 'I baptize you in the name . . .': these features had no place in the original western rite. Peculiar to the West were the triple interrogation on the faith and the post-baptismal ceremonies. The earliest clear and complete example of the western pattern is to be seen in the *Apostolic Tradition.* For the eastern pattern the earliest complete example appears in the baptismal instructions of St John Chrysostom; earlier examples are to be found in the *Testament of Levi,* the *Didascalia,* and the *Acts of Xanthippe and Polyxena,* but these reflect the rite at a stage before the development of the *apotaxis* and *syntaxis.* In the course of time, as the Church responded to pastoral needs and to the social conditions around it, as baptisteries and churches came to be built, as men were inspired to express their faith in prayers and hymns and other liturgical forms, these simple patterns became overlaid with a massive structure of accretions and elaborations, so that it is not always easy to detect their original simplicity beneath the complexities of the developed rites of Rome and Milan, of Antioch and Byzantium. Another consideration which influenced the development of liturgy was the communication which was maintained between the different regions where the Church flourished. Christians on journey or on pilgrimage, clergy and others on official or unofficial business, and the exchange of literature, all served to promote contact between the churches and to aid a process of cross-fertilization between the liturgies of different areas. We have noted in the previous chapter one important example of this process in the progressive adoption by the western Church of the eastern form, 'I baptize you in the name . . .'. Other notable examples are the process by which the eastern Church adopted an anointing after baptism where originally it had none, and the adoption of eastern features into the rites of Alexandria and Egypt although originally these were probably western in type.

The initiation rite of Antioch was clearly described by St John Chrysostom in about the year 388, and we have observed that it did not include a rite of anointing after baptism. However already at about that date, and probably a little earlier, a post-baptismal anointing is attested by the *Apostolic Constitutions* (DBL, pp. 31, 32, 34) and in the catecheses (DBL, pp. 29f) of St Cyril of Jerusalem. The catecheses (DBL, pp. 49f) of Theodore indicate that by the end of the century baptism at Mopsuestia was followed by a ceremony which included a signing with the cross and very probably an anointing, although Theodore is not quite specific on this point. All this evidence suggests that since a post-baptismal anointing was being adopted in the region of West Syria in the closing years of the fourth century it probably reached Antioch soon after the year 388. Dionysius the Areopagite is witness (DBL, p. 58) that it was firmly established there a hundred years later.

Elsewhere in the East the post-baptismal anointing made its way rather more slowly. A catechesis[20] written by Proclus, patriarch of Constantinople from 434 to 447, betrays no knowledge of it. However a letter[21] written by Gennadius, who was patriarch from 458, refers to the form 'The seal of the gift of the Holy Spirit'. In later years this was the form which accompanied the post-baptismal anointing in the Byzantine Church, as we see from the Barberini Euchologion, (DBL, p. 82) *c.* 790. But whether Gennadius knew of the form in that particular context is not certain, though perhaps probable.

In East Syria, the homilies of Narsai (DBL, pp. 52f) show that no post-baptismal ceremonies were observed at Edessa in the middle of the fifth century, but two hundred years later the revision of the Nestorian liturgy by the patriarch Isho'yabh included the addition of a ceremony after baptism. According to T. Thompson[22] this involved a signing with the cross in oil, but Thompson adds that the use of oil is generally omitted and the printed texts[23] of the Nestorian rite support this.

E. C. Ratcliff[24] conjectured that the post-baptismal anointing in the rites of the eastern Church originated with St Cyril and is to be attributed to western influence. Fisher[25] questions this, and points out that while the western anointing was on the forehead only, the easterns anointed on the forehead and on the organs of sense. However there is at least one point in St Cyril's rite which strongly suggests western influence. He says, 'Each one of you was asked whether he believed in the name of the Father and of the Son and of the Holy Spirit, and you made this saving confession and descended three times.' This is very reminiscent of the triple interrogation on the faith and its answers as we have noted them in the *Apostolic Tradition,* and other western sources. St Cyril is well known as an innovator in liturgical matters, notably in the development of the Church's year.[26] There is also reason to believe[27] that the eucharistic rite which he describes owes something to the Egyptian liturgy of St Mark. It is therefore difficult to resist the conclusion that St Cyril's baptismal rite is hybrid and not typically eastern. It shows its eastern character by the presence of an *apotaxis* and *syntaxis,* but also owes a debt to enrichments from the West of which the post-baptismal anointing may well be one.

Dom Bernard Botte[28] has gone further than Ratcliff by proposing a more precise explanation of the circumstances which led to the introduction of a post-baptismal anointing into the rite of West Syria. According to Botte, it originated in the requirements of the reconciliation of heretics, which was one of the preoccupations of the period. He begins by noting Canon 48 of the Council of Laodicea, which prescribes that after baptism candidates should be anointed with chrism. The date of this Council is between the years 380 and 450, and Botte conjectures that it took place in the early part of that period, at about the time, or soon after it, when the post-baptismal anointing was beginning to appear in the liturgical records of West Syria. Canons 7 and 8 of the Council are concerned with the reconciliation of heretics, some of whom were to be rebaptized and others not, according to the nature of their heresy. For those who did not need to be rebaptized, the canons prescribed that after they had anathematized their heresy and learned the creed, they were to be anointed with holy chrism and then celebrate the holy mysteries. Botte goes on to quote a letter written by Gennadius of Constantinople, in which Gennadius refers to the canons of Laodicea and fills them out with some detail. He says that those who are not to be rebaptized are to be anointed on the forehead, the eyes, the nostrils, the mouth, and the ears. 'In sealing them we say: *The seal of the gift of the Holy Spirit*.' This procedure is virtually identical with the post-baptismal anointing of the later Byzantine rite. But the context in which Gennadius writes suggests that it was originally designed as a suitable means by which to impart the Holy Spirit to heretics who were deemed to have been validly baptized but had not received the Holy Spirit. Since the early Syrian baptismal order had no distinct rite for the gift of the Spirit, the anointing was designed to provide one for circumstances when it was needed. 'After that it was only a step to extend the anointing to all the baptized. This is what the Council of Laodicea did.' Botte's theory is not necessarily inconsistent with Ratcliff's, and he acknowledges the possibility that the introduction of the post-baptismal anointing may have been prompted by western influence. It is not altogether clear from Botte's argument that the use of anointing in the reconciliation of heretics antedates its introduction into the initiation rite. But Botte provides a persuasive explanation of why and how such a considerable innovation should have been made in the initiation rite, and it depends on his conviction that the original order of the Syrian Church had no distinct rite for the gift of the Spirit other than the washing of baptism.

Our knowledge of the early baptismal rite of Alexandria is very limited. In his *Commentary on Romans*,[29] Origen said, 'According to the form traditionally delivered to the churches, we have all been baptized in visible water and in the visible chrism': and in his *Homily on Numbers*[30] he referred to 'Interrogations and responses' among matters which made up the baptismal rite. Dionysius of Alexandria also testifies to questions and answers at baptism in a letter preserved by Eusebius.[31] Scanty as these fragments of information are, they are sufficient to indicate that the rite of Alexandria included the interrogations at baptism and an anointing after baptism, and this may lead us to think that it was originally western in character. However, the later liturgical documents of Egypt indicate that a basically western rite has been enriched with elements which belong to the East. The *Canons of Hippolytus* (DBL, pp. 87f)[32] present a revised version of the *Apostolic Tradition* and are therefore fundamentally western. Nevertheless we find that by comparison with the *Apostolic Tradition* the renunciation has undergone the addition of an act of adherence to the Trinity, and the Syrian form, 'I baptize you in the name of the Father and of the Son and of the Holy Spirit', is to be integrated with the western interrogations and said at each immersion. The date and provenance of the *Sacramentary of Sarapion* (DBL, p. 83)[33] are matters of current debate, but its Egyptian origin is not in question. The presence of a prayer 'in regard to the chrism with which those who have been baptized

27

are to be anointed', and the petition in the prayer 'that they may be partakers of the gift of the Holy Spirit', indicate a western rite. But the prayer after the renunciation includes a reference to an act of adherence, and this suggests that the rite attested in this document also has been subjected to eastern influence. Finally, in the fully developed Coptic (DBL, pp. 91f) rite we find an order so overlaid with eastern elements that its western basis is scarcely discernible. In its atmosphere, its framework, and many of its details it seems wholly oriental. In particular we note the presence of a *syntaxis* and of the eastern form of baptism: and the prayer which accompanies the pre-baptismal anointing is to be found almost word for word in the developed rites[34] of Antioch. Nevertheless a few distinctively western features remain to show the original ancestry of this rite. The credal interrogations preserve a tenuous existence immediately after the *syntaxis,* the post-baptismal anointing is followed by an imposition of the hand: and according to one text[35] of the Coptic rite, at the communion of the newly baptized they receive not only the holy mysteries but also milk and honey, a custom which is otherwise attested (DBL, pp. 7, 10, 153f, 158, 222) for Rome, Milan and Africa, but not for the rites of the East.

3

The Catechumenate

The gospel was first preached to adults and it was adults to whom the appeal was first made that they should repent and be baptized. Whether infants were baptized from the first is a matter for debate, but it is not likely that the debate will reach any firm conclusion. The fact is that there is no clear and solid historical evidence to support either side. The most that can be said with certainty is that infant baptism was practised from the beginning of the third century. Tertullian bears witness to this in his treatise on baptism (DBL, pp. 85f) and he does not care for it. He wonders why godparents should run the risk that death might prevent them from keeping their promises or that they might find themselves saddled with an unresponsive god-child. And why should innocent children hasten to the remission of sins? Why again should heavenly things be entrusted to those to whom we should not entrust earthly things? Nevertheless, although Tertullian evidently disapproved of infant baptism, he makes it clear that it happened in his day. The *Apostolic Tradition* (DBL, p. 5) is equally clear. It says: 'And they shall baptize the little children first. And if they can answer for themselves, let them answer. But if they cannot, let their parents answer, or someone from their family. And next they shall baptize the grown men: and last the women.' At whatever date the Church first began to offer baptism to infants, it is certain that the customs relating to baptism developed with adult baptism as their purpose, and that if infants also were brought to baptism no particular accommodation was made for it in the service.

From the beginning the Church administered baptism to converts only upon certain conditions. Thus when the eunuch asked Philip if he might be baptized, Philip made a condition: 'If thou believest with all thine heart, thou mayest' (Acts 8.37). It was at all times necessary for the Church to be assured that the candidate had sincerely embraced the Christian faith, and that he had renounced his former habits of thought, belief and behaviour, before it was possible to bestow upon him the privileges and responsibilities of baptism. Accordingly the postulant for baptism was admitted first to be a catechumen (DBL, pp. 3, 109, 112, 154, 169f), that is to say, someone who was under instruction. He might remain as a catechumen, accepting the Church's course of preparation, for as long as three years, or his catechumenate might be only brief. Much depended upon the individual, and upon the circumstances. In the age of persecution the period was likely to be long; in the fourth and fifth centuries it was not more than a few weeks. The *Apostolic Tradition* sets out what must have been in most places the customary procedure for receiving a postulant as a catechumen in the age of persecution: 'Let them be examined as to the reason why they have come forward to the faith. And those who bring them shall be witnesses for them, whether they are able to hear.' On this occasion they are to be instructed to remain faithful to their wife or husband, or if unmarried to remain chaste. People in many kinds of occupation were told to give them up, or they would not be accepted. 'If a man be a sculptor or a painter, he shall be taught not to make idols.' An actor, a charioteer, a harlot, any one given to the worldly and wicked pleasures of the public games or gladiatorial shows, priests and teachers of idols, a charmer or an astrologer, must all be told to desist or be rejected. 'A magician shall not even be brought for consideration.' These and many more things were the subject of the enquiry made when a man was brought to the Church by a Christian sponsor, seeking baptism. The *Apostolic Tradition* continues: 'Let a catechumen be instructed for three years. But if a man be earnest and persevere well in the matter, let him be received, because it is not the time that is judged but the conduct.'

A feature of the life of the early Church which we need to

understand if we are properly to appreciate the catechumen's course of preparation was the *disciplina arcani,* or 'discipline of secrecy in religious matters', which the Church observed. During the age of persecution it was illegal even to profess to be a Christian, and very often therefore it was unsafe. In such circumstances Christians did not advertise the time and place when the Holy Eucharist or other religious meetings were to be observed, as we do today. The Church had not the public place in the fabric of society which it widely has today. On the contrary, it had some of the appearance of a secret society. Moreover our Lord had bidden the Apostles not to cast their pearls before swine. For these reasons every care was taken to exclude from the Eucharist any but the faithful. Even catechumens were not admitted to the actual performance of the sacrament, but only to the preparatory part of the service at which, then as now, the Bible was read and sermons preached. This first part of the Communion service came therefore to be known as the Mass of the Catechumens. When it was over, the catechumens were dismissed and the doors shut behind them, so that none but the faithful were present (DBL, p. 6) to offer the Church's intercession and to celebrate the Eucharist. This practice of secrecy manifested itself in a number of ways. The Apostles' Creed, for instance, was taught to catechumens under conditions of great secrecy (DBL, pp. 27, 155), and only at an advanced stage of their preparation. Although the Church in the ancient world was not slow to proclaim the Christian faith, yet they hesitated to reveal to the public gaze those things which they held most sacred. Just as great care was taken of sacred books and vessels (and many men were martyred rather than hand them over to persecutors), so great care was taken by Christian people in the early centuries to keep the sacred text of the Creed to themselves. For this reason it was taught to catechumens by word of mouth at a separate and special occasion, known as the *Traditio Symboli* (DBL, pp. 103, 110, 114, 123, 154, 159, 174, 227), or Delivery of the Creed. Before the words of the Creed were revealed to the catechumens

31

they were strictly cautioned that they were not to commit them to paper but to write them rather on the tablets of their heart. They were in no case to repeat the Creed to unbelievers or heretics, or they would deserve the name of traitor. Accordingly at the *Traditio Symboli* the Apostles' Creed was presented to them in a sermon clause by clause, and repeated several times in the course of the sermon so that they should have every chance of learning it by heart. They would not hear it said regularly at the Eucharist or other services, for neither the Apostles' Creed nor any other had been incorporated into the worship of the Church before the year 500, and only in a few places even then. The *Traditio Symboli* was the only public liturgical occasion when they would ever hear it so they had to learn it then without delay, and at another occasion, known as the *Redditio Symboli,* or Return of the Creed, they were to repeat it one by one in order to show that they had learnt it. Thereafter they were to use it as a private devotion 'to say to yourselves daily, before you sleep, before you rise from sleep, and have it in mind at all hours of the day'.

It is necessary at this point to interpose a brief note to explain that the Creed had a place at two distinct and separate parts of the Church's baptismal rites, and they ought not to be confused. As we have just seen, one occasion of it was the twin ceremonies of the Delivery and Return of the Creed. This was the first occasion in point of time, and the less important; it belonged only to the preparatory course. The second occasion when the Creed was used was the actual performance of the sacrament as it was done in the western Church. The triple interrogation, 'Dost thou believe in God the Father Almighty? etc.', to which we have referred earlier, is very probably the source of the Creed's origin. It belongs to the very heart of the sacrament, and probably originated, so far as its outline is concerned, in the time of the Apostles.

Just as the Eucharist was protected from a hostile world by a discipline of secrecy, so also was the liturgy of baptism and its preparatory ceremonies. Not even the catechumens knew what ceremonies would take place during their preparation, or in the actual performance of baptism, until they came to them. They were not explained to them in advance but in a course of addresses after the baptism had taken place. An example of this is found in the course of instructions given to catechumens by St Cyril of Jerusalem (DBL, pp. 24f) in the fourth century. The first series, known as the *Catecheses,* consists of nineteen addresses and their subject is Christian faith and behaviour. From the beginning, in the first address, they were warned not to divulge to the outside world the things which they would see and hear in the course of preparation. The second series consists of five addresses, known as the *Mystagogical Catecheses,* which were delivered after the baptism had taken place in the course of Easter Week, and in them St Cyril expounded the meaning of the various ceremonies which they had experienced. A similar series of addresses delivered by St Ambrose at Milan has also been preserved under the title *Concerning the Sacraments* (DBL, pp. 127f). At the beginning of this he explains: 'The Sacraments which you have received are the theme of my discourse. To have given a reasoned account of these earlier would not be right.'

The *disciplina arcani* was the natural response of the Church to a hostile world. Traces of it continued in existence long after the need had passed, so that even in eleventh-century Spain a sermon of St Augustine was still read at the Delivery of the Creed, commanding the catechumens, who would be infants, not to write down or repeat in public the words of the Creed. But in earlier centuries it was a necessary condition of the life both of the Church and of the catechumen.

The necessity for instructing catechumens in the true faith and sound devotional habits is obvious enough to the modern mind. It was plainly necessary to eradicate pagan belief from their minds and to fortify them against the errors of heresy. But there was another aspect of their preparation which to the mind of the early Church was of no less importance. To the early Church, as in the ancient world generally, possession by demons was a reality to be taken seriously. There were of course always a number of people in whom the signs of possession were evident and betokened by unmistakable physical symptoms. It was the view of the Church, however, that all men in whom the Holy Spirit had not made a dwelling must necessarily be possessed by the devil. It followed therefore that before the Holy Spirit could come to any one in baptism, the devil must first be driven out. John the Deacon (DBL, p. 155) expresses the matter admirably: 'There cannot be any doubt that before a man is reborn in Christ he is held close in the power of the devil: and unless he is extricated from the devil's toils . . . he cannot approach the grace of the saving laver.' Our next step therefore is to review the devices by which the Church sought to extricate men from the toils of the devil, which were regarded as an essential part of the preparation of the catechumen.

The practice of exorcism was common in the ancient world and it was certainly not originated by our Lord. 'If I by the Spirit of God cast out devils, by whom do your sons cast them out?', he asked. Plainly exorcism was customary among the Jews in his day, and his words seem to suggest as a possibility that it was not necessarily ineffective, although we know that it was sometimes performed by impostors. Basically an exorcism consisted of a solemn command to the devil to come out of the man. Christian exorcists made this command 'in the name of Jesus Christ', and would remind the devil of the coming judgement and of the pains of hell which he was to endure. In the western Church exorcists were a minor order of the clergy, solemnly admitted to their rank by the bishop, who handed to them at their admission a booklet containing the words of the exorcisms which they were to commit to memory (DBL, p. 227). The duties of exorcists lay both with those in whom the signs of possession were evident and also with catechumens preparing for baptism. Various actions, including the laying on of hands, were used to accompany the recitation of the exorcisms and heighten their solemn and awe-inspiring effect.

Periodic exorcism (DBL, pp. 25, 171) then, was one of the

devices by which the Church sought to expel the devil from catechumens, but it was by no means the only one. If we are to appreciate correctly the significance of fasting in the early Christian world, it is necessary to realize that it was understood as an apotropaic, that is to say, a device to turn away the devil. Thus Tertullian says of fasting: 'Christ taught that the battle against the worse kind of demons was to be carried out by fasting', and referred to our Lord's words: 'This kind cometh not out but by prayer and fasting'. This is in fact the original purpose of the fast which from an early date preceded baptism (DBL, pp. 1, 4) and which in due course developed into the forty days of Lent.

Another apotropaic was the sign of the cross. This sign was understood not only as the mark of a shepherd on his sheep but as a sign which the devil feared. So Narsai (DBL, p. 53) says: 'The cause of the signing on the forehead is for the confusion of devils.' St Augustine (DBL, pp. 99f) also taught that the sign of the cross had the same protective value as the blood of the Passover lamb upon the doorposts of the children of Israel.

Certain material substances, when a blessing or exorcism had first been pronounced over them, were also credited with apotropaic power. Foremost among these were oil, used for application to the body, and bread and salt, to be eaten. These things were commonly blessed or exorcized for use in ministry to the sick, to the possessed, or to catechumens. Until 1969, when the rite for infant baptism was revised, in the Roman Catholic communion salt was given to the infant before his baptism as part of the rite, and the prayer which accompanied its administration described it as 'salt, a saving sacrament to drive away the enemy'. This is a relic of a practice which at one time was a regular part of the discipline of the catechumenate, that periodically they received portions of salt or bread (DBL, pp. 99f, 113, 155, 170, 222). The fourth-century collection of prayers known as the *Sacramentary of Sarapion* (DBL, pp. 83f) includes one with the title, 'Prayer in regard to oil for the sick, or for bread or for water', and which has a plain statement of their apotropaic purpose: 'that it may become to those who are being anointed with it (or are partaking of these thy creatures) for a throwing off of every sickness and every infirmity, for a charm against every demon, for a separation of every unclean spirit . . .'.

Another apotropaic rite which was practised in the preparation of catechumens was a formal act of blowing upon the devil (DBL, pp. 143, 155). This is known as 'exsufflation', and was a common sign of contempt in the ancient world not confined to the practice of the Church or to liturgical occasions. People who were badly disposed towards the emperor might display their contempt by blowing upon his statue, and indeed there existed a law which treated such behaviour as treason. The significance of exsufflation in the preparation of catechumens is well explained by John the Deacon: 'And so he received exsufflation, because the old deceiver merits such ignominy.' Similarly a rubric in the rite of Milan reads: 'Blow upon him from head to foot to mock the devil.'

One other device to drive the devil away which we must notice is the act of renunciation spoken by the candidate. The renunciation, which remains in our Prayer Book service today, is one of the earliest developments in the baptismal rite and was used universally in the preparation of catechumens. It is important to appreciate that in its earliest form the renunciation appeared not as a question, 'Dost thou renounce the devil, etc?', but in the much more solemn and effective form of a declaration made boldly and directly to the devil himself: 'I renounce thee, Satan, and all thy service and all thy works' (DBL, pp. 5, 39, 114). The apotropaic character of this form was slightly weakened when it developed into the form: 'I renounce Satan, and all his works, etc.' (DBL, pp. 32, 47) and weakened still further when it was framed in the interrogatory form in which we know it to-day (DBL, pp. 128, 183). In some parts of the eastern Church the custom grew up of using an exsufflation to accompany the renunciation. Thus in the rites observed at Constantinople the candidates said: 'I renounce Satan and all

his works and all his angels and all his service and all his pomp.'
The priest would then command: 'Then blow upon him' (DBL,
pp. 70, 77). There is not much difference perhaps between
blowing upon the devil and spitting upon him. The practice of
spitting rather than blowing when the devil was renounced is a
late development in the eastern rite, and the earliest mention of
it is in a thirteenth-century manuscript of the Armenian rite
(DBL, p. 67). The evidence for such a practice on a liturgical
occasion in the West is very weak (DBL, p. 127) and uncertain.

4

Adult Baptism in the Western Church

When we speak of the baptismal liturgy we do not refer simply to the solitary event when the sacramental acts were performed. They are to be regarded as the culminating point of the baptismal liturgy, but the liturgy itself is the whole process spread over weeks or months or years, by which the candidate was gradually delivered from the power of darkness and translated into the Kingdom of God. In the previous chapter we examined the elements which made up the preparatory course of the catechumens and noted that they were devoted to two ends, the instruction of the candidate and the expulsion of the devil from him. Our purpose now is to see how these elements were co-ordinated in one coherent course and to set out the catechumen's progress from his admission until the day when his initiation was complete.

The date which we have in mind is roughly the century from 350 to 450 when the rites of adult baptism reached their fullest flowering. It is not possible to say precisely at what date the Christian faith was so universally accepted that adult baptism became a rarity, and that all candidates for baptism were infants. Plainly this was likely to happen at different times in different places, but in the great centres of the West there were probably few adults left to be baptized by the year 500. We may safely say that the 'peak period' for adult baptism was in the new age which was inaugurated in the year 311. In that year the Roman empire passed into the control of an emperor[36] whose mother was a Christian and who was himself at least favourably disposed towards the Church. Without delay the Church was placed on equal terms with the pagan religions, and in the years which followed Christianity came to be virtually the established religion of the empire. The long age of persecution was over. In such

38

circumstances as these, people who formerly might have hesitated to ask for baptism, fearing that it might lead to martyrdom, turned more easily to the Church. Every year large classes of candidates for baptism attended for instruction and preparation. The Church had the opportunity to develop her institutions without hindrance or restraint, and her liturgy represented a direct response to the contemporary situation.

The rites observed in the preparation of catechumens followed the same basic pattern in all the principal regions of the western Church, that is to say in Rome, Spain, Africa, France, Milan and North Italy, although the details varied from one region to another. In this study we shall concern ourselves more with the common pattern than with the regional variations. The first stage was that a person who sought to be baptized was admitted to be a catechumen. This might take place early in Lent, or it might be at any time. St Augustine gives an account of how a man should be treated who comes to his priest seeking to be admitted as a catechumen. He presents the occasion as a pastoral one, when the priest should give the postulant a first and general exposition of the Christian faith, and invite him to consider his decision carefully. If he is resolved upon his course he is to be formally made a catechumen in a ceremony of which the details vary from place to place. He would certainly be exorcized: he might receive an exsufflation. In Rome and Africa he would certainly receive his first taste of exorcized salt (DBL, pp. 100, 170). The liturgical books contain the necessary prayers and formularies for the performance of these ceremonies, as also for the imposition of the sign of the cross. This last feature of the admission of catechumens was common to all regions. It was above all by the sign of the cross that they were deemed to receive their new character as catechumens, no longer citizens of this world only, but already on the way to being members of the Church. By virtue of the sign of the cross they were already called Christians, and indeed in France the service which was generally called the Order for the Making of a Catechumen was called the Order for Making a Christian (DBL, pp. 160, 208).

The catechumen would be expected to attend the Mass of the Catechumens regularly, and there he would learn to establish himself in the company of the faithful and receive the instruction of bible readings and sermons. He was dismissed before the Eucharist began, but in Africa before he left he would receive at every service a morsel of salt (DBL, p. 222). At one stage this was probably the custom at Rome as well, for the salt which he received when he was admitted to be a catechumen was described at Rome as 'this first morsel of salt' (DBL, p. 170). So, just as the faithful received their sacrament in the Eucharist, so the catechumen had his own lesser sacrament in the salt. Thus, speaking of the salt, St Augustine says: 'And what they receive, although it is not the Body of Christ, is nevertheless holy, and holier than the food which we normally eat, since it is a sacrament.'

When the Lenten fast began it brought a severer discipline. The fasting itself, of greater or less severity, helped to turn the devil away, and to turn the catechumen's mind towards God. At the same time he would be required to attend special courses of instruction each day. One or more exorcists would be in attendance (DBL, pp. 25, 38) and every day when the class was ended they would lay their hands on the head of each catechumen and pronounce an exorcism over them.

The important occasions known as scrutinies (DBL, pp. 102, 106f, 112, 148f, 166-9, 229) must next engage our attention. In Africa one scrutiny of the catechumens was held, at Rome three, and they took place mid-way through Lent. But first it is necessary to correct a misunderstanding about the scrutiny which originated in ancient times and remains common today. From the word itself one might naturally suppose that the scrutinies were examinations designed to ensure that the candidate had followed his course of instruction carefully, and had learned the Creed, the Lord's Prayer and all other things which he ought to know. Already by the year 500 John the Deacon understood the word in this sense and supposed that this was the purpose of the three scrutinies of the Roman rite.

He says: 'Then follow those occasions which are commonly called scrutinies. For we scrutinize their hearts through faith, to ascertain whether since the renunciation of the devil the sacred words have fastened themselves on his mind: whether they acknowledge the future grace of the Redeemer: whether they confess that they believe in God the Father Almighty.' At a still later date the word 'scrutiny' came to be used of any of the seven occasions when children were brought to church in preparation for baptism. In fact however the original meaning of the word was something quite different, and was related not to the course of instruction but to the course of exorcism which had accompanied their instruction. In the process of preparation the catechumens had been exorcized many times: the purpose of the scrutinies was to ensure that the exorcisms had been effective and to satisfy the Church that no one was finally presented for baptism whom the devil still rendered unclean. Thus St Ambrose, in a sermon to catechumens after the scrutinies at Milan, said: 'Thus far the mysteries of the scrutinies have been celebrated. Therein search was made lest some uncleanness should still cling to the body of any one of you.' Similarly St Augustine, preaching in the same circumstances, said: 'Since we have ascertained that you are now free from unclean spirits, we congratulate you and admonish you that the health which has now been made evident in your body may be present also in your heart.' From each of these quotations we learn that the scrutinies were evidently concerned to demonstrate the cleanness of the body from the infestation of unclean spirits.

The scrutiny took place at night and was undoubtedly an ordeal for the catechumens who endured it. The following extracts from sermons by a bishop of Carthage, a contemporary of St Augustine, which were preached immediately after a scrutiny, give some impression of what happened.

The presence of so great an assembly demands that I explain to you the significance of the past night. . . . For our senses were not lulled with the delight of sleep nor our minds deceived with dreams . . . but in watching and praying, with psalms, in strife with our adversary the devil; we felt a great light flooding our hearts, and in the night we performed the works of the day. For what did we do in the night? We put the devil to flight and brought Christ in. . . . What was done in the night? Pride was destroyed, humility brought in, the chief of all evil was expelled and the fount of all goodness received.

What is it which in this night has happened about you that did not happen in past nights?: that from hidden places you were brought forward one by one in the sight of the whole Church, and then, with bowed head (which once had been held too high), with lowly feet, upon strewn sackcloth, examination was made upon you, the proud devil was driven out of you, and the lowly most high Christ was called down upon you. . . . If our help is in his name, let us renounce the devil, his pomps and his angels. You have heard this, it has indeed been your profession, to renounce the devil, his pomps and his angels.

All the sacraments which are wrought over you are wrought by the ministry of the servants of God, in exorcisms, prayers, spiritual songs, insufflation, sackcloth, bowing the head, lowliness of feet (DBL, pp. 106f).

From these three quotations, enigmatic though they may appear, we have more information about what happened at a scrutiny than from any other source. Supplementing them from other scraps of evidence, we may build up an account of the course of the occasion. It began late at night in a candle-lit church. The bishop was present with his retinue of priests and deacons and a large gathering of the faithful. The service began and continued for some little while with prayer and readings from Scripture interspersed with psalmody. At the appropriate moment the catechumens were withdrawn from the body of the church to some vestry or other room. There they were largely divested of the protection of their clothing, and particularly of their footwear, while in the church a goatskin or piece of sackcloth was spread on the floor and possibly strewn with ashes. Then from their hidden place, already perhaps tired with fasting, they were led out one by one and made to stand with their bare feet uncomfortably on the goatskin. This was well known in the ancient world as a symbol of sin, which they were to tread under their feet. Now, with the bishop and his clergy ranged on either side and with every accompaniment of solemnity, he was called upon first to renounce the devil, his pomp and his angels. This done, rebukes in the name of the dread Trinity were pronounced upon the devil, in exorcisms which were both lengthy and terrifying, and accompanied by exsufflations and the sign of the cross. Some few candidates must presumably have found the ordeal too great and broken down beneath it. They were deemed to be not yet freed from the toils of the devil and their baptism would accordingly be postponed to another year. The rest were led forward to receive an unction of oil, applied to the ears and nose, which was the last of the ceremonies of the night. According to John the Deacon (DBL, p. 156), this unction signified that their ears were now 'fortified so that they might permit entrance to nothing harmful which might entice them back', and that their nostrils were fortified so that they could 'give no admittance to the pleasures of this world, nor anything which might weaken their minds'. This was probably the original and primitive significance of this unction, and it meant that the rite was designed to close the senses against any further assault of the devil.

The performance of this final unction at the end of the scrutiny is probably the rite which developed into the ceremony known as the *Effeta* (DBL, pp. 113, 118, 122f, 128, 143, 183, 211, 216). The *Effeta* purports to be a liturgical performance of our Lord's miracle (Mark 7.32) when he healed a deaf-mute, touching his ears and mouth with spittle and saying Ephphatha (*Effeta*, that is, Be opened). According to our earliest account of the matter by St Ambrose, the priest who performed the *Effeta* touched the ears and *nostrils* of the candidate with *oil,* and said '*Effeta,* that is, be opened, unto an odour of sweetness.' The ceremony in fact is the same as that described by John the Deacon: oil was used to touch the ears and nostrils in his account. But it seems impossible that John was acquainted with the formula: '*Effeta,* that is, be opened.' It is quite clear from his words that to John the purpose of the ceremony was to close the senses, whereas this formula suggests that it is to open them. St Ambrose himself was evidently embarrassed by the discrepancies between the gospel account of the miracle and its liturgical performance. He gives a most unconvincing account of the reason why the nostrils have been substituted for the mouth (the impropriety of a priest touching a woman's mouth), and is so embarrassed by the use of oil rather than spittle that he avoids a specific mention of it, although it is clear that it was used. Liturgical history abounds with examples of actions with a practical and utilitarian purpose being clothed in a symbolism which is quite irrelevant. This appears to be one of them, and in this case the new symbolism was not merely irrelevant to the original purpose of the act but precisely contrary to it. Nevertheless in most of the developed rites of the West the *Effeta* appears immediately after the last and severest exorcism, just as it had concluded the final scrutiny. With the passage of time it was adapted more closely to the gospel story: spittle was substituted for oil in the Roman rite, and in Spain and North Italy the mouth was touched instead of the nostrils.

The catechumen who had emerged successfully from the scrutiny or scrutinies was fit to be entrusted with the words of the Creed. At Carthage, therefore, when the scrutiny was over and in the course of the Mass which followed, the bishop delivered a sermon in which he set the Creed before the catechumens. As we have said before, the Delivery of the Creed was one of the notable events of the preparatory course, and many sermons have been preserved which were delivered on the occasion, by St Augustine, St Ambrose, St Peter Chrysologus,[37] Nicetas of Remesiana,[38] and others. The Delivery of the Creed was a feature of the preparatory course which was common to all areas of the western Church, but the occasion of its Return has left little trace in the records, except that at Rome it took place at the last preparatory gathering on Easter Eve. However, one point on which the regions varied was that in some of them not only the Creed was delivered but also the Lord's Prayer. In Africa the Delivery of the Lord's Prayer took place on the Sunday after the Delivery of the Creed. Augustine expressly told his candidates that he is not so concerned about their memorizing this as he is about the Creed; they will have many chances of memorizing the Lord's Prayer, since they will hear it weekly at Mass after they have been baptized, whereas after their baptism they will never hear the Creed again. At Rome in a most impressive ceremony there was delivered to the candidates not only the Creed but also the Lord's Prayer and the Four Gospels.

The classes, the exorcisms, and the fastings lasted to the end of Lent, with the scrutinies and the Delivery of the Creed and so on as the public highlights of the catechumens' preparation. We may suppose that the last occasion when they were gathered together must have been invested with some particular solemnity, but in fact our records leave no trace of it except so far as Rome is concerned (DBL, p. 183). There the final preparatory occasion took place early in the morning on Easter Eve. Our account of it in the *Gelasian Sacramentary* is of relatively late date, and it is not clear whether it reflects accurately the course of the occasion as it would have been observed in the period under review. Thus according to the *Sacramentary* the first ceremonies of the gathering were an exorcism of impressive intensity beginning, 'Be not deceived, Satan', followed by the *Effeta*. But we have already seen that the *Effeta* was originally performed after the third scrutiny some weeks earlier, and must therefore infer that it has been transferred to Easter Eve as a later development.

The next ceremony at this gathering was the Renunciation. Probably this was done more than once in the preparatory course, and particularly at the scrutiny. Originally as we have seen it took the form of a declaration boldly made to the devil, but developed quite early into a triple question. The objects of the renunciation were originally many and various but finally were reduced to the devil, his work and his pomp. By the pomp of the devil two things have been understood. According to some writers it means his retinue, the lesser demons and agents of evil who serve him; others interpreted it in terms of the wickedness of the theatre and public spectacles and games. French and Spanish writers hint at a lengthy catalogue of the things renounced, including not only the devil but also his evil works, his worship and idols, sorcery and divination, pomp and theatres, thefts and frauds, fornication and debauchery and lies. Before the renunciation was made, but as part of the same ceremony, the breast and shoulders of the candidate were anointed with exorcized oil. The purpose of this was probably apotropaic, but St Ambrose (DBL, p. 118) places a symbolic interpretation upon it. He compares it to the preparation made by an athlete before going to wrestle: in the same way, he says, the Christian athlete is anointed before he wrestles with the devil.

The Return of the Creed followed, and the candidates ascended one by one to a platform from which they were to recite the Creed in the hearing of the faithful. This was the last act of their preparation and after prayers they were dismissed with the words: 'Dearly beloved brethren, go back now to your homes and await the hour when the grace of God shall be able to enfold you.'

In the evening of the same day the candidates assembled again in church with the faithful for the Easter Vigil. The night was spent in prayer and psalmody and readings (DBL, pp. 125, 184f) from the Old Testament. The lessons set out the eternal purposes of God, and the part which baptism and the Church plays in them. Beginning with the Creation, they continued with the story of Noah who was saved from perishing by water; of the children of Israel who were delivered from bondage and safely led through the Red Sea; of Abraham, and God's promises that he should be the father of many nations; and with readings from the prophets foretelling the mystery of the Church. Of the collects, one remains in common use to-day, beginning *O God of unchangeable power and eternal light.* All of them reflect the confidence and joy of the Church of the fourth century as she saw her numbers increased each year with new-born sons and daughters.

In the fourth century and for some time to come no font stood at the entrance to the church. The performance of the actual baptismal washing was carried out in relative privacy in the baptistery which was built beside the church. When the night's vigil was ended a litany was sung while the candidates and the bishop and his clergy moved in procession to the baptistery. There was no room there for the faithful, and in any case the baptism of adult men and women necessarily called for privacy; the faithful would remain in church at prayer. The litany ended, the bishop proceeded to the blessing of the waters of the font. In this lengthy prayer (DBL, pp. 119, 138, 160f, 186f, 209f, 217f) the bishop first invoked the presence of God and his blessing upon what the Church was about to perform. He called upon God to be faithful to past revelations of his power and by the Holy Spirit to give fecundity to the water, to purify the water and disperse all evil spirits which might infest it. As he made the sign of the cross over the water the bishop recalled God's act in separating the sea from the dry land, in providing water from the rock in a thirsty land, and finally our Lord's command to teach all nations and baptize them. The prayer ended: 'Here may the stains of all sins be blotted out, here may the nature which was founded upon thine image be restored to the honour of its origin and cleansed from the filth of age, that every man that enters this sacrament may be reborn in true innocence and new infancy.'

Some baptisteries at least were provided with cubicles built into the inside wall, and the candidates were now led from the cubicles one by one to stand in the water of the font. A deacon stood with him, and he or some other member of the clergy put to him the three questions:

Dost thou believe in God the Father Almighty?
Dost thou believe in Jesus Christ his only Son who was born and suffered?
And dost thou believe in the Holy Ghost: the Holy Church: the remission of sins: the resurrection of the flesh?

The exact details of these questions varied from place to place (DBL, pp. 5f, 121, 129f, 188, 211), but the reply to each was the same: 'I believe.' After each reply the deacon poured water over the head of the candidate, and after the third reply his baptism was complete. He came up from the font and another took his place.

We have noted in an earlier chapter that the practice of confirmation was the subject of much variation. At Rome in the fourth century, however, when the candidate was dressed and arrayed in shining white (DBL, p. 157) he was taken to where the bishop was now enthroned and as he knelt down the bishop laid his hands on him and recited the prayer for the sevenfold gifts of the Holy Spirit, which is still used in confirmation today. The bishop then signed him on the forehead with chrism, saying:

The sign of Christ unto life eternal.
℞ Amen.
Peace be with you.
℞ And with thy spirit. (DBL, p. 188)

When all were confirmed, the bishop and his clergy returned to the vestry, and the newly-baptized Christians, who are now to be called neophytes, or 'newly-born', went in their baptismal robes to join the faithful for the Easter Eucharist.

In order to complete our account of adult baptism as it was practised in the early Church in the West, it is necessary to treat of a number of ceremonies which followed baptism. The first of these is known as the *pedilavium* or washing of the feet (DBL, pp. 104, 130, 142, 162, 212, 221, 223). At an early date, not later than the third century, the custom had grown up in some places that the bishop who presided over the baptism washed the feet of the candidates after they had been baptized. While this was being done, the appropriate passage from St John's Gospel was read, of the occasion when our Lord washed the disciples' feet, anthems were sung, and the bishop gave a charge to each candidate: 'I wash thy feet as our Lord Jesus Christ washed his disciples' feet; do thou even so to pilgrims and strangers'. As an encouragement to the practice of Christian humility and service, this was an excellent and edifying ceremony, and it was upon this understanding of it that the Gallican Church maintained the ceremony for many centuries. Unfortunately, however, a different interpretation came to be placed upon it, which caused it to be confused with the sacramental washing of baptism. Thus we find St Ambrose teaching that just as a man's own sins were washed away in baptism, so the washing of the feet washed away the hereditary sins which he derives from Adam, whose feet were tripped by the serpent. This elevated the washing of the feet from a useful and edifying ceremony to a level on an equality with the sacrament of baptism itself. Teaching of this kind had originated no doubt before St Ambrose's time. As early as 305 we find a council of Spanish bishops forbidding the practice, or at least forbidding the clergy to perform it themselves. Rome would have nothing to do with it. St Augustine approved of the practice for the lesson that it teaches, but recognized with sympathy that in many places its performance was transferred to some other occasion in order to avoid any confusion with baptism.

It is most probable that in the age of persecution the clothes which a candidate assumed after his baptism were the same as those which he had taken off before. There is certainly no evidence to the contrary, except perhaps from Syria. But in the fourth century the practice became universal that when he dressed after baptism he put on white liturgical vesture and head-dress (DBL, pp. 49, 56, 58, 66, 97, 115, 122, 157, 162, 203, 220, 247). This must have contributed greatly to the festal character of Easter, for it was to be worn at the Easter Eucharist and all other liturgical occasions throughout the week. John the Deacon interpreted the white vesture in a number of ways. For one thing, it symbolized the resurgent Church. He also says: 'They wear white raiment so that though the ragged dress of ancient error has darkened the infancy of their first birth, the costume of their second birth should display the raiment of glory, so that clad in a wedding garment he may approach the table of the heavenly bridegroom as a new man.' The white head-dress in particular, he says, is a symbol of the priesthood which they now share with all Christians: 'for priests of ancient time used to deck their heads with a certain mystic covering'. Apart from its symbolism, however, the head-dress in the West served the practical purpose of protecting from defilement the chrism with which the bishop had anointed the neophyte's forehead, and hence it came to be known as the *chrismale,* or chrisom-cloth. By the Middle Ages the vesting of the infant neophyte with white robes had all but been given up, and all that was left was the chrisom-cloth, white bands tied round the forehead over the chrism. Even then, however, the charge continued to be given in France and elsewhere which ran: 'Receive this white garment and bear it stainless before the judgement seat of Christ.' The custom still continued in England during the brief currency of the Prayer Book of 1549. The rubrics of that book provided that white vesture should be put on the child, with the charge: 'Take this white vesture for a token of the innocency . . .'. But it is very probable that in most cases the white vesture was no more than a white band around the head.

The other custom to be recorded was the practice whereby at the Easter Eucharist the celebrant not only consecrated bread and wine for Communion, but also blessed a cup, or cups, one of milk and honey (DBL, pp. 7, 10, 153, 157, 222), the other of water. These were communicated to the neophytes at the same time as the eucharistic species themselves. They were interpreted as a symbol of the entry into the promised land which flowed with milk and honey. It is very probable, however, that they represent the last traces of the meal of which the Eucharist was originally a part. The custom seems to have fallen out of use with the disappearance of adult candidates and the declining popularity of Easter baptism.

5

The Sarum Rite

Our study of the baptismal liturgy as it was normally performed in the fourth century has revealed a rite or a process which was spread over at least several weeks, and which revolved around Easter and Lent. Even at this date, however, there were certain factors which called for a rite more like that which we use today, a brief service of about twenty minutes' duration, in which everything necessary was accomplished. One of these factors was that in appropriate cases the Church did not deny admission to the dying or to those who it was feared might die. In such emergencies it was deemed necessary that they should first be admitted to be catechumens with the customary ceremonies, the exorcism, the first morsel of salt, the sign of the cross, and the prayers which went with them. Then it was as necessary with the candidate on the sick bed as with any one else that before he was baptized and became a dwelling of the Holy Spirit, room should be made for the Holy Spirit by the expulsion of the devil. So the customary apotropaic rites needed to be employed, exorcism, the *Effeta* and the renunciation among them. The course of instruction plainly had to be abandoned; all that could be briefly reproduced of that was a recitation of the Creed. Then finally the candidate on the sickbed was baptized as he answered the interrogations upon the Creed, or as someone else answered them for him. By the performance of all these things one after another, the whole of the initiatory process which normally was spread over a lengthy period was telescoped into the compass of a half-hour's performance (DBL, pp. 192-4).

Another factor which encouraged the development of a brief rite such as this was the declining popularity of Easter baptism, and the sense of unreality which must have been felt when the lengthy initiatory process was performed over a catechumenate which consisted exclusively of babes in arms. The same process continued to occupy the Church through Lent until Easter for several centuries. In theory parents were expected to bring their children to church early in Lent to be made catechumens; to bring them on several other occasions during Lent to be exorcized and to receive the Creed, the Lord's Prayer and the Four Gospels; and last of all on Easter Eve to be baptized and confirmed (DBL, pp. 196-204). The worshipping Church was spared the intrusion of these matters upon their Sunday Mass, and the meetings were transferred from Sunday to Monday: this is the ancient equivalent to what today is deservedly censured as 'hole in a corner' baptism. We shall not be surprised if rightly or wrongly parents preferred to have their children baptized with less trouble.

In the Prayer Book of 1549, Archbishop Cranmer introduced the rubric which says: 'It appeareth by ancient writers that the sacrament of baptism was not commonly ministered but at two times in the year, at Easter and Whitsuntide', and hints that the custom might very well be restored. Of course what the Archbishop said is true: we have just seen that Easter was the normal occasion for baptism in the fourth century, and we may add here that Whitsuntide was the occasion when any were baptized who for reasons of health or other good reasons missed the Easter baptism. Nevertheless, the Archbishop's statement calls for certain qualifications. In fact, the practice of Easter baptism did not become universal very early and it did not last very long. We cannot say how early the practice may have originated in some part or other of the Church. The earliest clear evidence is that of Tertullian, who said: 'The Pascha affords the most solemn occasion of baptism. . . . After that, the fifty days of Pentecost [sc. Easter] provide the most extended season for conferring baptism. . . . However, every day is the Lord's; every moment is apt for baptism.' This is sufficient evidence that Easter baptism was customary in Africa about 200, but it is not lightly to be assumed that the practice was universal in the West, perhaps for another fifty or a hundred years. It is astonishing to observe how quickly the practice began to decline. A letter exists, written by Pope Siricius before the end of the fourth century to Himerius, bishop of Saragossa, to say that he had heard of baptism being performed at Christmas and on the feasts of martyrs, and condemning the practice. Fifty years later Pope Leo wrote to the bishops of Campania and Picenum in similar terms. Protests of the same kind were made at Councils at Gerona in 517 and at Auxerre (DBL, pp. 225, 228) in 578, and at the latter Council it was resolved to forbid baptism at any other time but Easter, except for the dying. But it is plain that the tide of popular opinion had turned against the requirement that the baptism of infants, who were now the great majority of the candidates for baptism, should be delayed until Easter, and that they should be treated in identical fashion with adult candidates and required to appear in church time and again throughout Lent. In spite of all the efforts of Popes and Councils, the eighteenth Canon of the second Council of Macon (DBL, p. 229) in 585 complained pathetically that 'at the holy Pascha only two or three children can be found to be baptized'. By force of habit, the ancient customs of Lent and Easter were maintained for some centuries in a slowly attenuating form. But the practical business of the Church in administering baptism was carried on all the year round, on Sundays and feast days, and for this purpose a relatively short order of service was a necessity.

The Sarum Order of Baptism (DBL, pp. 231ff) is an example of the short order of service which developed in response to these considerations. The reader should not be dismayed if upon a first reading it appears hopelessly confused and chaotic; upon examination it will be found that in fact it is not without coherence and order. However, from the fourth-century rite which we studied in the last chapter to the Sarum rite on the eve of the Reformation there is a gap of a thousand years, and in order to bridge that gap there is one further aspect of liturgical history which needs to be explained. We have pointed out before that every region had its own liturgical customs, and that although the basic pattern of the baptismal liturgy was the same everywhere, the details were not. A thousand years later the baptismal liturgy, like the Eucharistic, was virtually the same throughout the western Church. There were still differences between the services employed in different places, but they were very much less. The reason for this progress towards uniformity is that over the thousand years of which we are speaking the practices of the Roman Church had been steadily adopted by all the other Churches of the West. This happened only partly because of the Roman claim to hegemony and authority in the West. It is certainly true that the Roman Church did in some measure seek to impose her liturgical practices on other Churches. But it is also true that bishops in all parts of the West responded freely to the Roman claims with requests for advice on liturgical and other matters. Moreover, it was genuinely necessary to preserve liturgy from heresy and eccentricity, and this has something to do with the disappearance of the rites of Spain and the substitution of the Roman rites. In France a century or more of war and turbulence had thrown the liturgical and ecclesiastical institutions of the Church into chaos, and when peace and order were restored under Charlemagne the Gallican Church was glad to turn to the books of the Roman rite for help in restoring an orderly liturgy. And so it was throughout the West that the local practices of the various regions were largely abandoned and the Roman liturgy put in their place. This happened in England also and the Sarum rite is fundamentally the rite of the Roman Church. Nevertheless, and this is important to the analysis of the Sarum rite, local customs were not totally forgotten or abandoned. Small points of local tradition were often retained and fitted into the framework of the Roman rite. Moreover, orders of service never remain quite static, and it was inevitable that the rite should gain some accretions over the centuries. And so we shall find in the Sarum rite that, while the framework is Roman and consists of prayers and ceremonies which had been in use in

Rome since the fourth and fifth centuries and possibly earlier, yet this framework is partly overlaid and partly obscured by a number of matters which had been preserved from local custom and a process of accretion.

A first and superficial analysis of the Sarum order of baptism shows that it is divided into three sections: the Order for making a Catechumen, the Blessing of the Font, and the Order of Baptism itself. It will be convenient to examine the last of these first. We find at the heart of this section the sacramental act, that is to say the triple washing accompanied by the baptismal formula; and immediately before this comes the triple interrogation upon the Creed, which as we have seen was itself the original baptismal formula of the western Church. The position of the credal interrogation as we see it here is the position which it had held without any single exception in all the baptismal rites of the western Church since the Syrian formula was adopted; for although with the adoption of the Syrian formula the credal interrogation ceased to be the essential formula in baptism, it never lost its place in the closest association with the performance of the sacrament. Gathered about the sacramental act we find also a number of other rites, the renunciation, the presbyteral unction, the giving of white robes, and the giving of a candle. We observe that the renunciation is still accompanied by an unction applied to the breast and shoulders of the infant, just as it was in the fourth century: but in the interval the unction has acquired a new and uninspired formulary to accompany it. The renunciation is really out of place in this section of the rite. At Rome it belonged to the preparatory course and was performed among the rites of the morning of Easter Eve. However the Gallican Church in France and Spain had early been attracted by the formal similarity of the triple interrogation upon the Creed and the triple interrogation of the Renunciation, and had drawn the two together, so that the presence of the renunciation in this part of the Sarum rite, in close association with the sacramental act, is a legacy of the Gallican Church. The unction which follows baptism in the Sarum rite belongs to the most ancient practice of the Roman Church. It was always performed by a priest and is not to be confused with confirmation (DBL, pp. 6, 188, 203f). While the dressing in white robes was a normal practice of the Church since the fourth century, the Roman rites prescribed no formularies for the purpose, and the charge in the Sarum rite is another legacy from the Gallican Church. The early customs of the Church have no precise counterpart to the giving of a candle to the neophyte, although the carrying of candles by the candidates for baptism or by the faithful in procession to the font sometimes added a touch of colour and pageantry to the observances of Easter Eve. But in the form in which it appears in the Sarum rite, the giving of a candle to the neophyte and the charge which accompanies it may be regarded as characteristic medieval accretions, first attested in the eleventh century.

The prayer for the Blessing of the Font is the same prayer that had been in use in the Roman Church in the fourth century. It was the work of the Gallican Church, however, to elaborate it by providing the *Sursum Corda* as an introduction. The Litany which precedes it reminds us of the processional approach to the font in the fourth century. We must note that the rubrics do not require the blessing of the font at every performance of baptism but only as often as was necessary to maintain the cleanliness of the water. It follows that on some occasions the administration of baptism would begin with the order for the making of catechumens and then go straight on to the third section and the performance of the sacrament.

We turn now to the Order for Making a Catechumen. This has been elaborated over the centuries with a number of additions, not always very intelligently made, but basically its design is a recapitulation of the ancient preparatory course of catechumens in the Roman Church. The prayers and ceremonies for the admission of a postulant to the catechumenate have been preserved exactly as they had been for centuries. First there is the prayer, 'Almighty, everlasting God, Father of our

57

Lord Jesus Christ, look upon this thy servant N., etc.', followed by the sign of the cross and a collect. Then the salt is exorcized and administered and this act is followed by an appropriate prayer. This completes the admission of a catechumen. Then follows a series of exorcisms and related prayers, first over male candidates and then over female, although the differences in the prayers do not seem to be in any way related to the distinction of the sexes. This series consists for the most part of prayers and exorcisms which had been used at Rome since the fourth century and ends with the prayer, 'O Lord, holy Father, everlasting God of light and truth'. These exorcisms represent the regular exorcisms of the preparatory course and also the scrutinies at which the efficacy of the exorcisms was tested. Finally we may identify the observances of the last gathering of the catechumens on the morning of Easter Eve. These, we may recall, consisted of the exorcism 'Be not deceived, Satan', accompanied by the *Effeta,* the renunciation, and the Return of the Creed. In the Sarum rite, as we have seen, the renunciation has been transferred to a later stage, but the other elements of this last gathering of the catechumens remain. We note that as well as reciting the Creed the priest is also to recite the Lord's Prayer and the Hail Mary.

Now that we have identified the basic design of the preparatory section of the Sarum order, it is possible to indicate the accretions which it has collected. First there is the ceremony which stands at the very beginning of the rite when the priest makes the sign of the cross upon the brow and breast of the infant, with two uninspired formularies provided to accompany the act. This does not belong to the original rite and only detracts from the significance of the sign of the cross in the section which follows. Secondly, we note that the gospel reading describing our Lord blessing the children has been inserted between the exorcism, 'Be not deceived, Satan', and the *Effeta.* The gospel had been used in the Gallican Church in connection with the preparatory occasion, some weeks before Easter, when children were brought to church for exorcism and unction.

These rites involved the laying of hands on the infants' heads, and this gospel was therefore thought to be appropriate to the occasion. Thirdly, the signing of the cross upon the right hand of the infant was a rite of some antiquity (DBL, pp. 220f). Finally, the formula, 'Enter the temple of God, etc.', which is not of Roman origin, confirms the instructions of the rubrics, that the whole of the preparatory section of the rite is to take place at the church door.

It remains to clear up a minor point of difficulty and explain that the title of the first section, which describes it as the Order for Making a Catechumen, is a misnomer. It is in fact another example of the failure of the medieval Church to understand the significance or coherence of the rites which they administered. The title is apt enough for the ceremonies which stand at the beginning of the section, the signing with the cross and the administration of salt. These things belonged to the occasion when a heathen was accepted as a catechumen. But the various matters which follow in this first section of the Sarum rite belong not to the making of a catechumen but to his subsequent discipline and preparation.

6

The Prayer Book Orders
of Infant Baptism and
Confirmation

No one who has carefully studied the Sarum order of baptism
will be surprised that the Reformers took radical steps to amend
it. Solemnly to commence proceedings by making a child a
catechumen was not a realistic thing to do. Again, while even
the modern mind might accept a single exorcism in the rite as
an appropriate act of preparation for baptism, the Sarum rite
was too much encumbered with prayers and ceremonies with an
apotropaic purpose; and if this apotropaic purpose had in some
instances been forgotten, as it probably had with the salt and the
Effeta, no good purpose or sense had been substituted for it. It
was also to be expected that some attempt would have been
made to amend the interrogations. As they stood in the Sarum
rite they were unreal, because they were addressed to an
uncomprehending infant; and the answers on the face of it are
not altogether honest, since they make statements which are
plainly untrue. For it is simply not true to say that an infant
renounces the devil or that he believes in God, and the only
excuse for the statement is that they were commonly interpreted
as promises for the future.

Many centuries earlier, in Africa, France and Spain, some
attempts had been made to adjust the interrogations, which
originated in the circumstances of adult baptism, to the
requirements of infant baptism. Thus there is evidence that St
Augustine (DBL, p. 105) asked the godparents: 'Does this child
believe, etc.?'; this is a shade less unreal than addressing a
question directly to an uncomprehending child. Similarly there
is a manuscript of the Spanish rite (DBL, p. 121) which provides
the form: 'I baptize him in the name, etc.', which also avoids the

unreality of a direct address to the infant. The same manuscript goes further than this, and as an answer to the question 'Dost thou believe, etc.?' it supplies the answer 'He shall believe', instead of the customary 'I believe'. A solitary French manuscript (DBL, p. 211) proposes as an answer to the same question the reply *Credat,* which means literally 'Let him believe', or less literally 'Let us pray that he will believe'. But these isolated attempts to introduce reality and truth to the rites of infant baptism had been obscured by the widespread adoption of the Roman rite, and by the time of the Reformation they had long been forgotten.

A superficial examination of the order of Public Baptism in the 1549 Prayer Book reveals the same triple division which we found in the Sarum rite. The first part, as in the Sarum rite, is carried out at the church door. The Blessing of the Font is the next section, although in the book of 1549 it is actually printed among the regulations for 'them that be baptized in private houses in time of necessity'. Again as in the Sarum rite this is not necessarily to be used at every occasion of baptism but 'once a month at the least'. The third section is concerned with the sacramental performance and with those other ceremonies which in the Sarum rite had accompanied it. It is astonishing to notice how little change Archbishop Cranmer made in this section of the rite. The triple renunciation has lost the unction of breast and shoulders which had accompanied it from ancient times; the ceremony of giving a lighted candle to the neophyte has disappeared; the presbyteral unction now follows the giving of the chrisom, instead of preceding it. Otherwise this, the most important section of the rite, remained substantially as it had been before, with the triple renunciation and the credal interrogation preceding the sacrament, and the giving of the chrisom and the presbyteral unction following it. The prayers for the blessing of the font are shorter than the litany and lengthy prayers of the Sarum rite and owe little to it. They have been shorn of all the ceremonies which accompanied the blessing of the font in the medieval order.

The most important changes, however, are those which have been made in the first section of the rite. Here Cranmer has retained from the Sarum rite the crossing of the child, on the brow and breast, although the formula which accompanies it is new, and there is nothing to indicate any purpose to make the child a catechumen. He has retained also an exorcism and a prayer to accompany it from Sarum. The gospel narrative of our Lord blessing the children which in Sarum was taken from St Matthew's Gospel appears now in its Marcan form. The sermon which follows it leads by a devious route to the recitation of the Lord's Prayer and Creed, so that the last traces of the ancient *Redditio Symboli* are thus preserved. The last debt to Sarum of this introductory section of the 1549 book is the invitation of the priest as he leads the child from the church door to the font: 'The Lord vouchsafe to receive you into his holy household.' For the rest, the giving of salt, the multiplicity of exorcisms, the *Effeta,* and a host of smaller matters have been thrown on the scrap-heap. In their place Cranmer has introduced certain material of a more edifying kind which he borrowed from the reformed baptismal rite drawn up in Germany for Hermann, Archbishop of Cologne, and known commonly as 'Hermann's Consultations'. This material provides the prayers and hortatory passages of the rites which are commonly criticized today because they make the rite a dreary and lengthy monologue by the priest. Any one who will study the text of Hermann's Consultations (and they are very difficult to come by, for such an important document) and observe its heavy verbosity will learn a new respect for Cranmer as a master of brevity and lightness. It must be acknowledged that in doing away with so much of the ancient material of the Sarum rite the Archbishop performed a service which was long overdue. It is, however, unfortunate that whereas the first section of the Sarum rite for all its faults had at least a fairly coherent framework, which was probably not understood, the comparable passage of the 1549 rite lacks any scheme or structure such as might bind its separate elements into a coherent unity.

The Prayer Book of 1552 reflects the Reformers' passion for doing away with all outward observances which were not strictly essential, and for creating rites heavy with the didactic and hortatory character which was then deemed to be most edifying. In 1552 the whole service was directed to be held beside the font. The exorcism, the chrisom and the presbyteral unction were dispensed with. The prayers for the blessing of the font were retained, but with the vital difference that the key phrase which called for the sanctification of the water was omitted, so that what was left was simply a prayer for the candidate. The only inessential ceremony to be preserved from antiquity was the sign of the cross. The consequence of this wholesale abolition of ancient custom, which began in 1549 and was completed in 1552, was that practically nothing was left of the old rites. To be precise we may specify that what remained was the prayer *Almighty and immortal God,* the gospel, the interrogations, and the sign of the cross, and it is to be noted that even these were employed in entirely new contexts. It is therefore quite mistaken to attempt to trace any substantial relationship between the rite of Sarum and the rite of 1552. The service of Cranmer's second Prayer Book is virtually a new creation, and it is as such that we must examine it. A century later in 1662 this order of service was revised and reached the form in which we use it today. In spite of certain differences between the orders of 1552 and 1662 they are structurally and substantially the same and may therefore conveniently be examined together.

The baptismal rite of the Prayer Book has this much in common with that of Sarum, that it falls naturally into three sections; and also that, as in Sarum, the second section is for the blessing of the font, and the third is occupied with the sacramental act. We naturally consider the third section first, as we have done throughout this study, because that is the point on which all else is focused and which gives significance and purpose to everything else. We note first of all that apart from the Lord's Prayer, another prayer appropriate to the occasion, and the charge to the godparents, this section consists only of the sacramental washing, the baptismal formula, and the sign of the cross. The sign of the cross has been brought to this position, not inappropriately, from its original position at the beginning of the rite. We recall that in ancient times it was the most significant ceremony in the making of a catechumen at the beginning of the preparatory course. Now it is used as a suitable sign made upon the baptized person to declare something of the character of the baptized life. But it is *not* part of the sacramental act. The second thing which we notice about this section of the Prayer Book order is that the credal interrogation is missing from its ancient position in association with the sacramental act. We recall that once it was actually the baptismal formula, and that it had always been used in close association with the performance of the sacrament. There was reason in the association. Baptism is a covenant between God and the person who is baptized. God's blessings are bestowed in the sacramental act; man's part in the covenant is declared in the credal interrogations. The two things in association thus express the baptismal covenant in a most fitting manner and it is therefore unfortunate that the questions have been moved from this position. The fact that the renunciation has also been moved is of less importance, for originally it had no place there and logically it is more appropriate in the preparatory section.

The blessing of the font stands between the introductory section and the performance of the sacrament; in 1662 the invocation calling upon God to sanctify the water was restored to the prayer. It should be noticed that the prayers for the blessing of the font consist of the four short prayers beginning, 'O merciful God, grant that the old Adam in these children, etc.', and the longer prayer which follows them. On the face of it the four short prayers may appear to be an appropriate pendant to the interrogations which precede them. Historically speaking, however, we may see that all these five prayers, together with certain others, appeared in the book of 1549 as part of a longer devotion for the blessing of the font, and that they have been inserted into the Prayer Book order as one unit. Moreover it becomes clear upon a more careful examination that the phrase in the fourth of these prayers, 'whosoever is here dedicated to thee by our office and ministry', looks forward to the sacramental act and not backwards to the questions and their answers. It follows that if a hymn is introduced into the baptism service to cover a procession to the font, it should come before these four short prayers and not after them.

The first section of the Prayer Book rite opens with an address and two prayers which establish a context of devotion for the sacrament. The entire passage which follows, beginning with the gospel reading and ending with the interrogations, form one coherent unit, and the concept which gives it coherence is that of covenant. The business of this passage is to set out the promises which are exchanged between God and the candidate. Accordingly when the gospel has been read an address follows, which first interprets the gospel as an assurance to doubtful parents of God's readiness to receive the child, and then, after a prayer, as a declaration of God's promises to receive the child, to release him of his sins, to sanctify him, and to give him the Kingdom of heaven. We may think that as an interpretation of the gospel reading this is rather far-fetched, but it is undoubtedly what the Prayer Book says. After this declaration of God's promises, the child is now required to make *his* promises, and to this end it is the business of the priest to ask the child the four questions and of the godparents to supply the child's lack of articulate speech and make his answers for him. At this point we should notice an ambiguity or inconsistency which Cranmer has introduced into the rite. The answer to the questions in the Prayer Book order remain as untrue as they always had been in the context of infant baptism. But the effect of this is modified because in certain passages of the rite they are spoken of not as statements of present fact but as promises for the future. This inconsistency has resulted in much confusion in the understanding of the rite. However by these means the covenant is set out declaring first God's promises and then the promises of the child. The necessary preliminaries have been completed and it is thus possible to proceed first to bless the waters and then to baptize the child.

In order to complete our study of the Prayer Book order of infant baptism it is necessary to examine in detail the four questions which we have called in general the interrogations. The first thing about which it is important to be quite clear is that they are all addressed to the child. This is made perfectly clear by the third question, 'Wilt thou be baptized in this faith?' which can only be addressed to the child; to suggest that this question alone is asked of the child and that the other three are put to the godparents is simply irrational. However it is more important to know who is bound by these questions and their answers than to determine who is asked them. Since the Reformation there has been dispute about this point, whether it is the godparents who should bind themselves on their own account to renounce the devil and to believe in God, or whether it is the children who should be thus bound. The interrogations in Hermann's Consultations are clearly designed to bind the godparents but not the child. Similarly, when the revision of the Prayer Book was under discussion in 1660 the puritan faction demanded that the promises should be made by the godparents on their own account. That is why the phrase 'in the name of this child' was introduced into the first question in the 1662 Prayer Book. It is designed as a deliberate answer to the Puritans to make it clear that the promises or statements which the godparents speak are made in the name of the child and not on their own account. But this phrase was not new in 1662. It appeared already in 1552 in the order for Private Baptism, and thus makes it clear that in 1552 also, in spite of a rubric which directs that the questions should be put to the godparents, the promises were to bind the children.

It must be confessed that the introduction of the phrase 'in the name of this child' raises a difficulty. If as we have said the questions are in fact put to the child, then this phrase seems out of place and pointless. It seems unreasonable to say to a child,

'Dost thou in the name of this child . . .?' The solution of this problem can only be to understand the phrase as an interjection addressed to the godparents, while the rest of the question is addressed to the child. In effect the priest is saying to the child, 'Dost thou renounce the devil . . .?', and turning to the godparents he interjects the reminder, 'Remember that your answers are not made on your own account but in the name of this child.'

It remains to note two other passages in the service which indicate quite clearly that it is the child who is bound by the promises and not the godparents. In the address which precedes the questions, we find the words, 'This child must also faithfully for his part promise . . .', and in the charge to the godparents at the end of the service, 'Forasmuch as this child hath promised . . .'. These passages have the double interest both that they make it clear that the promises are the promises of the child and not his godparents, and also that they introduce the future tense into the rite. The questions which the child answers through his godparents are answered in the present tense and are therefore, as we have observed, not strictly true. These passages introduce the idea of a promise for the future, and we may interpret the interrogations and their answers in the light of them. The idea of promise in this context appears also in the catechism of 1549 ('They did promise and vow three things . . .'), although oddly the third promise, of obedience, was not added to the baptismal rite until 1662.

The changes which were made at the Reformation in the performance of confirmation were as follows: the ancient prayer for the seven-fold gifts of the Spirit was retained; the use of oil was abolished and replaced by the imposition of hands; and the formula which had accompanied the unction was revised to suit the laying on of hands. In addition to these important changes, the prayer with which the Sarum rite had ended was replaced with another borrowed from Hermann. According to the old practice the oil had been administered by the bishop with his thumb in the sign of the cross. The book of 1549 which abolished the oil preserved the sign of the cross immediately before the imposition of hands, but in 1552 the sign of the cross was also abolished, and the formulary again changed to that which remains in use today. The purpose of these changes was to bring confirmation more closely into line with biblical precedent.

The importance which the reformers attached to confirmation may partly be judged from the rubric in the 1552 book which assures us that no harm can result from deferring confirmation because 'it is certain by God's word that children being baptized have all things necessary for their salvation and be undoubtedly saved'. It follows that confirmation is not necessary to salvation, nor an essential part of the Christian life, and there is nothing in subsequent revisions of the Prayer Book which seeks to alter this doctrine or to contradict it. Nevertheless the reformers appear to have valued the imposition of the bishop's hands, partly no doubt because it appeared to accord with apostolic practice, but more particularly perhaps because it was now linked with the instruction of children, and its administration was made conditional upon their instruction. Before the Reformation godparents had been instructed at the baptism to see that their godchildren were taught the Creed, the Lord's Prayer, and the *Ave Maria,* but the probability was that the children would be confirmed some time before they were able to receive instruction, which was likely to be meagre if it was not quite neglected. In 1549 for the first time it was laid down that before they were confirmed children must learn by heart the Creed, the Lord's Prayer, and the Decalogue, and also answer questions from the catechism. In the books of 1549 and 1552 the manner in which the catechism is printed beneath the heading 'Confirmation', and before the actual order for confirmation, distinctly suggests that children were to be catechized, by the bishop 'or such as he shall appoint', as part of the service. The fourth question in the catechism, 'Dost thou not think that thou art bound to believe and to do . . .?', and its answer serve the purpose of a confession by the candidate of his baptismal vows, suitably made at such a time. Already therefore we see the confirmation service, which in the Sarum rite had been occupied exclusively with the administration of the sacrament, acquiring the two-fold character which it has today, consisting first of the renewal of the baptismal vows and then the laying on of hands with prayer. In 1662 the catechism was detached from the order of confirmation and replaced by the single question in which the bishop asks for a renewal of the baptismal vows; and at the same time the formulary beginning 'To the end that confirmation may be ministered to the more edifying . . .', which in 1549 had appeared as a rubric in the Prayer Book, was turned into the address with which the service begins.

7

The Initiation Services of the Alternative Service Book

The need to revise the initiation rites of the Prayer Book and especially the order for infant baptism has been recognized by the Convocations and the generality of the Church of England for forty years or more. As long ago as 1938 a joint committee of the Convocation of Canterbury reported that 'there is a great need for a revision of the service for the ministration of public baptism to infants'. This view was endorsed in subsequent reports entitled *Confirmation Today* (1944), *Baptism Today* (1949), and *Baptism and Confirmation Today* (1955), and by the opinions of the parish clergy in their deanery synods which are recorded in these reports. The reports are concerned primarily with pastoral and theological matters. They discuss the meaning of confirmation and its theological relation to baptism, the propriety of deferring baptism, the necessity that the clergy make good use of the pastoral opportunities which baptism provides, the breakdown of the institution of godparents, the age of confirmation, and other matters relating to pastoral discipline. Since at that date there did not seem to be any immediate prospect of liturgical revision, these reports make no specific recommendations about new orders of service, and their main liturgical interest is to press for more dignity and ordered ceremonial in the administration of the Prayer Book rite. Nevertheless certain points of dissatisfaction with the Prayer Book services do emerge. As long ago as 1911 Bishop Frere[39] had claimed that the order of infant baptism should be based on the order of adult baptism which ought to be primary, and not the other way round as the Prayer Book orders were framed. He had also propounded the view that the ancient unity of baptism, confirmation, and first communion should find

70

expression in a new order. Bishop Frere's views were faithfully reproduced in the Convocation reports. The reports also reveal much concern about the passages in the Prayer Book which appear to suggest that baptism conveys the remission of actual sins to infants. The vows in baptism were another matter of concern: some believed that the parents should commit themselves in the vows as well as the infants, others claimed that infants could not and should not be committed by them. The possibility that the use of chrism might be introduced was also mooted. Little was said in these reports about the gospel reading in the Prayer Book service. However the Lambeth Conference of 1958 proposed a list of elements which need to find liturgical expression in a new rite. This included 'the ministry of the word, declaring the teaching of Scripture concerning baptism'; it gave a list of appropriate passages, and the omission of Mark 10.13f from this list is noteworthy. Finally, the language and literary character of the Prayer Book was a common matter for criticism, and the reports express the urgent need for something shorter and simpler.

The revision of the Canons of 1604 began in the years immediately after the second world war and carried with it the hope that Parliament might approve a new procedure for liturgical revision such as would secure greater freedom for the Church of England in providing alternative forms of worship. This was the hope which inspired the Convocations when in 1951 the Convocation of York, responding to the evident demand, published the text of a proposed order for infant baptism, and in 1955 the Convocation of Canterbury included texts for the baptism of adults and infants and for confirmation in its report *Baptism and Confirmation Today*. Again in 1958 the Liturgical Commission, which had been appointed by the archbishops in 1954, published the first fruits of its work in a report entitled *Baptism and Confirmation*. However at that date there was still no ready means by which these proposals could legally be adopted for use in the parishes. It was not until the Prayer Book (Alternative and other Services) Measure had passed into law in 1965 that it became possible for the Church of England to secure liturgical reform without recourse to the lengthy procedure in Parliament which brought about the traumatic experience of 1928. No time was lost in taking advantage of the measure, and in 1967 the Series Two orders of baptism and confirmation were approved for experimental use. In 1971, when the revision of the Series Two orders was already under consideration, the General Synod received a report from a commission which had been appointed by the archbishops to consider the pastoral and theological problems concerned with confirmation and the admission to Holy Communion. This was the Ely report, named after the bishop who had been chairman of the commission, and its title was *Christian Initiation: Birth and Growth in the Christian Society.* The effect of the report and the debate which followed it was to focus attention on the need for a new service of thanksgiving after childbirth and on the need to recognize that baptism ought to be followed by instruction and training for responsible Christian life; and also to ask the bishops to consider the possibility that children might be confirmed at an earlier age than has been customary. The effect of this long debate on the revision of the Series Two services, which was eventually approved for inclusion in the Alternative Service Book, was therefore much more modest than this important report had called for.

In the following pages it is not our purpose to trace in detail[40] the evolution of the text of the initiation services as they appear in the Alternative Service Book or to compare them with the text of the Series Two services, but to comment on them as they are. It is necessary therefore to understand that like the rest of the contents of the Alternative Service Book the orders of baptism and confirmation are not the work of one individual. For better or for worse they are the product of a democratic process. The first step in the process was the preparation of a draft. This was the work of the fifteen or more members of the Liturgical Commission. Then, before it could be submitted to the General Synod, the Commission's draft had to be submitted to the House of Bishops and amended to meet their comments; and this was no mere formality. The text agreed with the House of Bishops was then presented to Synod, which appointed its own revision committee. This committee was free to disregard the opinions not only of the Liturgical Commission but also of the House of Bishops, and it did not hesitate to do so; there are a number of points where the revision committee restored to the final text what the bishops had taken away from the original, and there are others where the committee rejected the expressed views of the Liturgical Commission.

Pastoral need is an important spur to liturgical reform, and the new orders of service are designed to meet the criticisms of the Prayer Book rites which we have already examined, and to take account of the Ely report and of pastoral conditions in the twentieth century. The language of the new services of initiation, as of the whole of the Alternative Service Book, is one of the most notable contributions to this endeavour. 'You-form' is the language of worship in which children are now brought up in most schools in the country, and it is the language of worship in the modern liturgical books of the Roman Catholic Church and other Christian bodies. If the Church of England had persisted in the 'thou-form' of the Prayer Book, its worship would soon have seemed not only archaic but also eccentric. The introduction of 'you-form' made it necessary also to discard such archaisms as 'seest', 'moveth', 'vouchsafe', and 'forasmuch as'. But the most important feature of the new style of English is the replacement of sentences which in the Prayer Book are long and involved by sentences which are short and of which the meaning is clear; and the new initiation rites are not burdened with the long and tedious homilies which characterize the corresponding services of the Prayer Book. Such changes as these do not require the Church to abandon a high standard of English. Nor do they cause us to abandon our sense of reverence or of the solemn majesty of Almighty God, for these depend not so much on the words we use as the way in which we use them and the spirit which we bring to them.

Not all parents today are careful to bring their children to baptism, and some are careful to see that their children are not prematurely committed. It was necessary therefore to take account of a situation in which children are brought to baptism who have passed their infancy, and in which the decrease of infant baptism has led to an increase in adult baptism. This explains why the service for the 'baptism of infants' has given way to a service for the 'baptism of children', and why provision is made in the rubrics and text of the new services for occasions when the candidates are children in the region of seven years old. It also explains why it seemed important to provide for occasions when adults might be baptized and confirmed in one service, and why provision is made for 'household baptism'. The institution of godparents has ceased to be an effective way of ensuring the care of infants in spiritual matters. The new orders place the responsibility where it normally belongs, on the parents themselves, but without excluding godparents. They recognize also that the local congregation is not without responsibility for the nurture of the Church's children, and draw attention to this both in the address to parents and godparents and in the prayer which follows the ministry of the word. Care has been taken to indicate that as baptism is a spiritual birth it ought to be followed by spiritual growth, not only in the case of infants but also of adults. Members of the congregation are also reminded to be thankful for their own baptism and given the opportunity to pray that they may be faithful to it.

The new services adhere to the spirit of the Prayer Book rubric which requires that baptism is administered only at Morning or Evening Prayer on Sundays and Holy Days 'when the most number of people come together'. This rubric has been widely neglected, and the canons of 1964/9 are less rigorous on the subject. In any case the main Sunday service today in many parishes is the Eucharist. Accordingly the rubrics of the new services allow for a variety of use, but the services themselves are based on the assumption that they will normally be performed in the presence of a full congregation.

As churchpeople have become more conscious in recent years of the significance of baptism and of the importance of their own baptism, the possibility that they might renew their baptismal vows at intervals and not simply once in a lifetime at confirmation has increasingly captured their imagination. In 1956 the Roman Catholic Church included provision for the renewal of baptismal vows by all members of the congregation at the Easter vigil. This innovation was not essentially different from the annual 'Covenant service' which John Wesley instituted among the Methodists. Accordingly the Alternative Service Book provides an order for the renewal of baptismal vows which might be used in the course of the Easter vigil, at the New Year, or at any other suitable time, and the confirmation service includes an opportunity for members of the congregation to renew their vows in the course of the service.

The Church needs constantly to adapt its liturgy to changing circumstances, or it will come to seem irrelevant and unreal. But it needs also to be faithful to its past history and liturgical tradition, or it will cease to be true to itself or to the communion of saints in which it believes. This does not mean that it must slavishly copy every detail of past liturgy in the spirit of the antiquary or the curator of a museum. It means that we must examine the tradition in order to distinguish between the essential and the inessential, the constant and the ephemeral, and consider how best to preserve the constant and essential features of the tradition in forms suitable to our own generation. This explains why the structure of the new rite is not essentially different from the pattern of the western rite as we have observed it in its early stages. At the heart of the service there is the baptismal washing. This is accompanied by the 'form' which the western Church long since adopted from a Syrian source; and the ancient triple interrogation on the faith, which once constituted the 'form' of the original western rite, is also preserved in close association with the performance of the sacrament. In preparation for the sacrament we find the ancient renunciation at the heart of the Decision, which is followed by the prayer for the blessing of the water, and after the baptism the post-baptismal ceremonies which have characterized the western rite from an early date are still preserved.

By comparison with the Prayer Book rite we observe three major structural changes. Alone among all the manifestations of the baptismal liturgy in the western Church the Prayer Book detaches the interrogation on the faith from the sacrament itself, placing it before the blessing of the water among the preliminaries of the rite. The new services correct this, so that the questions on the faith come immediately before baptism. The second important change is the creation of the passage called The Decision. The effect of this is to detach the questions of the renunciation from the questions on the faith. As we have observed in an earlier chapter, it was not a sound development when the two series of questions were united in one. They are concerned with separate matters, they originated in isolation from each other, and each gains in its impact if it is kept apart from the other. The establishment of the Decision made possible the third important change by which the signing with the cross has been restored to a position in the preliminary part of the rite. The Prayer Book position had the unfortunate consequence which Cranmer cannot have anticipated that people have tended to suppose that the signing with the cross is the essential action in baptism. This mistaken view seemed to be supported by the fact that the priest holds the baby in his arms as he makes the sign of the cross. The ceremony was not inappropriate in the position to which Cranmer assigned it, for it illuminated something of the meaning of baptism. But it is no less appropriate in association with the renunciation. It is a sign of commitment with Christ in the struggle against evil and also of victory. It identifies the candidate with both, and the renunciation is the best place for it. Historically this position approximates more closely to the use of the signing with the cross in the Prayer Book of 1549 and earlier examples of the western baptismal rite, where it was associated with exorcism and other ceremonies concerned with the Christian's fight against evil.

The place of the Decision as a preliminary to baptism corresponds to St Peter's exhortation, 'Repent and be baptized' (Acts 2.38). Repentance is acknowledged to be the necessary preliminary to baptism, but in the New Testament 'repentance' looks two ways, both backwards and forwards. It means both repentance of past evil and also repentance 'unto life', it involves the concept of turning from one thing to another. So in the Decision the candidate affirms that he turns towards Christ and then as a consequence that he turns away from evil. This New Testament concept of repentance is fully represented in the first and last questions of the Decision. The second question does not seem to add anything to them and might well be discarded.

It is to be noted that the questions are to be answered by the parents and godparents 'for yourselves and for these children'. This combines the ancient tradition enshrined in the Prayer Book by which the children are credited with the answers made by their godparents with the new insight of the Reformation that the parents and godparents ought also to be implicated in the questions.

The section of the new services entitled The Baptism begins with a prayer said over the water. This indicates that since the preliminaries have now been completed the priest may approach the water and prepare for the baptism. In the comparable prayer in the Prayer Book water is mentioned only as a symbol of cleansing. The prayer ignores the other traditional associations of water in baptism, and so draws particular attention to the forgiveness of sins which in infant baptism is the least considerable of the functions of the baptismal water. In the new prayer water is presented as a symbol not only of cleansing but also of death and of new life. These three functions of water in daily life are shown to be its function also in the history of salvation, in the Old Testament, the New Testament, and in baptism itself.

The interrogations on the faith are related to the three Persons of the Trinity, as they always have been in the western rite. They are not concerned only with assent to intellectual propositions, for the candidate is asked not only whether he believes in the three Persons but also whether he trusts in them. The questions include an account of the work which we associate with each of the three Persons, but the account is not altogether satisfactory. It is not enough today to speak of God's creative work as though it belonged only to the past, or of the work of the Holy Spirit as though it was limited to the people of God. Lapses like this are an inevitable consequence of the democratic process.

After the triple interrogation the new services have a congregational expression of faith. This is an innovation in the baptismal liturgy which the Church of England has borrowed from a similar form of the Roman Catholic rite of 1969. The triple interrogation is addressed to the candidate, who is the one primarily concerned, and it is not for the congregation to make the answers. This new addition enables the congregation to associate itself with the candidate in his profession.

The Prayer Book catechism associates the naming of a child with his baptism, stating that we are given our name by 'my godfathers and my godmothers in my baptism'. Consistently with this the Prayer Book service directs the priest to say, 'Name this child'. These features of the Prayer Book have encouraged a popular impression that the purpose of bringing a child to baptism is that he should be given a name. It is possible that in the Middle Ages baptism did sometimes (DBL, p. 144) provide the occasion when a child was named, though not at the very moment of baptism. In most cases today the name of the child has already been determined and commonly used when his birth is registered in accordance with the law, and in the case of adult baptism the candidate has had a name for some years and does not commonly change or amend it at his baptism. When St John Chrysostom attested the form 'N. is baptized, etc.', he did not suggest that a name was then being given; the name used would be the name by which the candidate had long been known. Similarly in the sixth century the *Gelasian Sacramentary* is witness that the children were enrolled by name at the beginning of the preparatory course some weeks before their baptism. Considerations of this kind[41] are the reason why the rubrics of the new services avoid the suggestion that the child is being named at baptism, and require only that the officiant shall address the candidate by name.

St John Chrysostom described (DBL, p. 41) the expressions of delight which took place after baptism in the fourth century. He said, 'As soon as they come forth from those sacred waters, all who are present embrace them, greet them, kiss them, rejoice with them, and congratulate them.' Spontaneous demonstrations of this kind may not come easily to us today as our formal rites follow their appointed course, but the giving of a lighted candle and the welcome are designed to express the same emotions. The giving of a candle is of medieval origin, first encountered[42] in an eleventh-century Missal and attested (DBL, p. 247) in the Sarum rite. The welcome replaces more fully the Prayer Book words, 'We receive this child into the congregation of Christ's flock', which may prove misleading if they suggest that reception into the Church is effected by signing with the cross.

Attention has already been drawn to the controversy which surrounds the rite of confirmation. To put it briefly, some believe that this is a sacrament conveying the Holy Spirit, others believe that it is not a sacrament and does not strictly speaking convey anything. Proponents[43] of each belief have suggested that both points of view might be accommodated if the imposition of the hand were to follow immediately after baptism, in the baptism of infants as well as of adults. This would be a return to the practice which is at least as old as the *Apostolic Tradition,* and it would avoid the need to assign different benefits of Christian initiation to different parts of the total rite (or so it is claimed). It would involve the consequence that the imposition of the hand could no longer be reserved to bishops, since they could not be present on every occasion when a child was to be baptized. This was the most fundamental matter discussed by the General Synod in its debate on the Ely Report, and since Synod reached no theological conclusion and declined to make any considerable change in pastoral practice, it was left to the Liturgical Commission to draft rites of baptism and confirmation which observed a theological neutrality, not favouring either point of view to the exclusion of the other.

The doctrinal standards of the Church of England are set out in the Book of Common Prayer and the Thirty Nine Articles, and these combine to suggest that confirmation is not a 'sacrament of the gospel' comparable to baptism and the Eucharist, but that it is an occasion to pray that the candidate, who has received the Holy Spirit in baptism, will be strengthened by his gifts. This reflects Cranmer's belief[44] that 'the bishop in the name of the Church doth invocate the Holy Ghost to give strength and constancy with other spiritual gifts unto the person confirmed, so that the efficacy of the sacrament is of such value as is the prayer of the bishop made in the name of the Church'. Effect is given to this approach to confirmation in the central petition of the prayer for the seven-fold gifts of the Spirit, which reads, 'Strengthen them with the Holy Ghost and daily increase in them thy manifold gifts of grace'. In the new services an important change has been made at this point. The central petition is now cast in the words of scripture (Isa.11.2 RSV) to read, 'Let your Holy Spirit rest on them', in an endeavour to provide a prayer which does not favour either party in the controversy. This is not to say that the prayer is theologically empty. On the contrary, it carries with it the positive teaching that the Christian has entered the new age of the Messiah which Isaiah foretold, and that he has received the full outpouring of the gifts of the Spirit; only it does not attempt to indicate the point at which this outpouring takes place, whether it is to be associated with the water of baptism or with the laying on of hands. A similar neutrality is observed in the form of words which accompanies the laying on of hands. This is shorter than the Prayer Book form as a matter of convenience, and it can be understood in a variety of ways.

The rubric provides that the bishop 'lays his hand' (singular) on the head of each candidate. This follows the Prayer Book which also has the singular number, and the Prayer Book in turn follows the unvarying terminology of the western Church in this respect. The fact that Anglican bishops usually lay both hands on the candidate's head, and that the rite is often known as the 'laying on of hands', very possibly springs from the common association of confirmation with the occasion when Peter and John laid their hands on the Samaritan converts and they received the Holy Spirit (Acts 8.17). The Prayer Book itself suggests this association when it says that hands are laid on the candidates 'after the example of the holy apostles'. But we have seen reason to doubt whether this passage in Acts is related by an unbroken tradition from the apostles to the later practice of the western Church in the imposition of the hand. It was the presence of this passage in the 1928 confirmation service which in 1966 led the House of Laity to refuse to authorize that order of service among the Series One services.

The Notes at the beginning of the initiation services allow that oil may be used at the signing with the cross in baptism and the laying on of the hand in confirmation. The Liturgical Commission had expressed the belief that a development such as this should be delayed until it had been further considered, for there is no point in ceremonies of which the meaning is neither apparent nor agreed. However the General Synod ignored this advice, and we are left to interpret the meaning of the oil by the words which are said when it is administered. The prayers for blessing the oils would help us to understand their meaning, but no such forms have been included in the Alternative Service Book. Where the signing with the cross is concerned we may presumably follow St Ambrose and interpret the anointing as that of an athlete about to wrestle in the fight of this world, which accords with the spirit of the Prayer Book words at the signing with the cross. When oil is used at confirmation, we should probably compare it with the oil with which priests and kings were anointed in the Old Testament, as an indication that in Christian initiation we enter a royal priesthood. But it is doubtful whether this ancient symbolism of the Mediterranean world is apparent or meaningful to the majority of English people today; it would need a great deal of explanation in sermons and other occasions for teaching. And, as J. D. Crichton has said[45] about the use of oil, 'as soon as you have to be told that this "signifies" that, you are being told at the same time that the symbol is dead'.

8

The Roman Catholic Initiation Rites
1969-1972

The edition of the *Rituale Romanum* of 1614 formed the
conclusion of the revision of liturgical books which was
instituted by the Council of Trent, and remained virtually
unaltered until 1964. It included two rites of baptism, one for
adults and the other, a slightly abbreviated version, for children.
These were not essentially different from the Sarum rite which
we have already examined. They preserved the gift of salt, the
exorcisms, the anointings, the delivery and return of the Creed,
the *Effeta,* and other matters which had originated in a very
different world centuries earlier. One of the most important
consequences of the Second Vatican Council was the
promulgation in 1964 of the Constitution on the Sacred
Liturgy,[46] and the effect of this on the initiation rites, as on all
other rites of the Roman Catholic Church, was profound and
speedy. But the revision of the rites which the Constitution
called for was not the result of a sudden, unconsidered, decision.
The renewal of liturgical study known as the Liturgical
Movement began in the middle of the nineteenth century,
fostered first by individual scholars and then by monastic
foundations and papal authority, and was at first concerned to
promote the active participation of the laity in the worship of
the Church. Scholars pointed to the fact that the liturgy of the
early Church in Rome was Greek in the early centuries, since
the common language was then Greek, and only changed to
Latin when Latin became the accepted vernacular, in order that
people could still participate in the rites. The conclusion was
obvious, that the liturgy should again be changed to the accepted
vernacular, which is no longer Latin. This was only one of the
many results of liturgical study over several generations which

the Constitution finally endorsed. Among the first fruits was the promulgation of the *Small Ritual, being extracts from the Rituale Romanum, in Latin and English.* This was scarcely, if at all, different from the Ritual of 1614, but it did provide for the use of the English language, in the administration of baptism as in other matters.

The Constitution on the Sacred Liturgy sets out in broad outline the principles which a revision of the initiation services ought to follow in order that they might promote both the edification of the faithful and the mission of the Church. Importance is first attached to the consideration that the faithful should understand the liturgy, with the consequence not only that the language should be understandable but also the other features 'which have rendered their nature and purpose (i.e. of the sacraments) far from clear to the people of today'. The catechumenate was to be restored, in several distinct stages. The rite for the baptism of infants was to be revised and adapted to the circumstance that the baptized are in fact infants, and the roles and duties of parents and godparents were to be brought out more clearly in the order of service. Except during Eastertide the baptismal water was to be blessed within the rite of baptism. 'The rite of confirmation is to be revised; the intimate connection which this sacrament has with the whole process of Christian initiation is to be more clearly set forth; for this reason it is fitting for candidates to renew their baptismal promises just before they are confirmed.' Provision was to be made that the administration both of baptism and confirmation might take place in the context of the Eucharist.

In obedience to the requirements of the Constitution, the Latin *Editio Typica* for the baptism of children was published by the Vatican in 1969, that for confirmation in 1971, and that for the Christian Initiation of Adults in 1972. Official translations into English followed soon afterwards.

THE BAPTISM OF CHILDREN 1969

The medieval rite indicated three different places at which the baptism service was conducted. It began at the entrance to the church, then moved inside the church, and was completed at the font or in the baptistery. Similarly the 1964[47] rite began outside the church door, continued with a procession to the font, and was completed in the baptistery. The new order allows more latitude. It provides that the reception of parents, godparents, and children may take place either at the church door or else in 'that part of the church where the parents and godparents are waiting'. The service then moves to the place where the Celebration of God's Word is to be performed (if they are not already there), and for this part of the service the infant candidates may be removed to a crèche. Then after the exorcism the congregation moves to the baptistery. But if the baptistery cannot accommodate the congregation, the baptism may be celebrated at a suitable place within the church, that is to say, at a basin or portable font in a convenient place. Finally there is a procession to the altar for the Lord's Prayer and the blessing.

The service begins with The Reception, and an inquiry about the child's name. This is a sufficient indication that the child is not named in baptism, and is in full accord with ancient practice. The question may be, 'What name do you wish to give your child?', or it may be, 'What name have you given your child?'. The parents next acknowledge their responsibility for the spiritual care of their child, and the godparents their duty to help them. The child is then signed, first by the priest, then by the parents, and then 'if it seems appropriate' by the godparents. The giving of salt has no longer any place in the rite. The Ministry of the Word consists of one reading from the Gospels, or two, a psalm, and a short homily, and is followed by the Prayer of the Faithful, for the infants, their parents and godparents, and all the baptized. After this the infant candidates, who may have been in 'a separate place' for the Ministry of the Word, are brought for the Exorcism and Anointing before Baptism. The exorcism does not take the ancient form of an address to the devil commanding him to depart from the child: it takes the form of a prayer that the child may be delivered from evil. It is followed by the anointing of the child on the breast with the 'oil of catechumens' and an imposition of the hand, although the local conference of bishops may decide to omit the anointing. J. D. Crichton, as we have seen, considers[48] this anointing to be a meaningless symbol today and therefore dead, and wishes that it might be omitted. But he does not extend the logic of his argument to cover the anointing after baptism and at confirmation. The service then moves to the font or baptistery, and several forms are provided for the 'Blessing and Invocation of God over the Water', which is to be used at all times except in the Paschal season. The questions of the renunciation and the profession of faith follow in one continuous series. This is an unfortunate departure from the ancient Roman practice, preserved in the 1964 rite, which recognized that the renunciation and the profession of faith are separate matters and kept them separate. In the 1964 rite the renunciation was the last part of the service before the entry into the baptistery, and it was only after the renunciation that the priest replaced his purple stole with a white one and then entered the baptistery. A more suitable place for the renunciation in a revised rite would be in association with the exorcism.[49] An important new development in the performance of the interrogations is that they are addressed to the parents and godparents and not to the child. It is the parents and godparents who are to renounce evil and profess their faith. But this faith is described also as the faith of the Church, and as the faith into which the child is to be baptized. By an imaginative innovation, the congregation then gives its assent to the profession of faith, acknowledging that the faith of the Church is the faith which they also are proud to profess.

After the baptism itself, three and possibly four post-baptismal ceremonies are performed. The anointing with chrism is a sign to show that baptism is an entry into the royal priesthood. The clothing with a white garment follows, and the intention is that this shall be a real garment and not simply a chrisom cloth. It is to be 'the outward sign of your Christian dignity'. A member of each family then lights a candle for each child: this is to show that they are 'to walk always as children of light'. The fourth ceremony is the *Effeta,* and this is used only 'if the conference of bishops decides to preserve the practice'. (The bishops of England and Wales have left the matter to the discretion of the local clergy.) The celebrant touches the ears and mouth of each child with his thumb. Saliva is not used. The accompanying formula interprets the action in the light of Mark 7.31f, and prays that the Lord Jesus may 'soon touch your ears to receive his word, and your mouth to proclaim his faith'. This ceremony bears little relation to the *Effeta* of past history and has strayed a long way from its ancient place in the rite. Finally there is a procession to the altar for the Lord's Prayer and the blessing.

The Ritual sets out separate orders for the baptism of several children, the baptism of one child, the baptism of a great number of children, the baptism of children by catechists, baptism of children in danger of death, and an order for bringing children to church after baptism. It also includes an appendix of alternative forms for the Ministry of the Word, the Prayer of the Faithful, the Exorcism, the Blessing of God over the water, prayers and acclamations, and the final blessing.

CONFIRMATION 1971

The main sources from which we may discern the official teaching about confirmation are the text of the rite itself, which includes a homily; the introductions to the rites of baptism and confirmation, which are concerned with matters practical, pastoral, and theological; and above all the Apostolic Constitution on the Sacrament of Confirmation delivered in 1971 by Pope Paul VI.

Confirmation is described in the Constitution as a sacrament and its form and matter defined. 'The Sacrament of Confirmation is conferred through the anointing with chrism on the forehead, which is done by the laying on of the hand, and through the words: *Accipe Signaculum Doni Spiritus Sancti.*'

The Constitution goes on to add that the extension of the hands over the candidates (now described as the 'Laying on of *hands*') which accompanies the prayer for the sevenfold gifts of the Spirit, 'does not belong to the essence of the sacramental rite', but 'contributes to the integral perfection of that rite'. The definition of the sacrament itself identifies the anointing and the laying on of the *hand* as one action, although the rubrics of the rite itself say nothing about the hand but require that the chrism is applied by the thumb only in the sign of the cross. A clear distinction is made, and the Constitution is explicit on this point, between the laying on of hands which precedes the sacrament and the laying on of the hand which is essential to it.

Up to the present time the form of confirmation has been, 'I sign you with the sign of the cross and anoint you with the chrism of salvation, in the name of the Father and of the Son and of the Holy Spirit.' This can be traced to the Roman Pontifical of the twelfth century. The new form is the ancient formula of the Byzantine rite and has been judged preferable. The translation into English of this form was at first a matter for debate, and this explains the various translations to which reference[50] is made by contemporary writers. However in October 1973 the Holy See intervened to settle this debate and reserved to itself the approval of all translations of sacramental forms. The translation of the form of confirmation which was then finally adopted was 'N., Be sealed with the gift of the Holy Spirit'. This form appears to carry with it the implication that the Holy Spirit is bestowed in confirmation, and this is consistent with other passages both in the Apostolic Constitution and in the rite itself. However some commentators point out that the meaning attributed to baptism is so full and rich that confirmation can add nothing to it, but can serve only to make explicit what has already been done in baptism; and draw attention to passages at many points in the documents which suggest that confirmation conveys some 'plus value' (a booster dose) rather than a new and original gift.

The Apostolic Constitution traces confirmation to our Lord's own institution, and many familiar passages of the New Testament are cited in support of this. 'The apostles, *in fulfilment of Christ's wish,* imparted the gift of the Holy Spirit to the newly baptized by the laying on of hands to complete the grace of baptism. . . . This laying on of hands is rightly recognized by Catholic tradition as the beginning of the sacrament of confirmation.' The difficulties posed by the early eastern rites of initiation are met by an assurance that 'a rite of anointing, not then clearly distinguished from baptism, prevailed for the conferring of the Holy Spirit'.

Section 71 of the Constitution on the Sacred Liturgy required that the 'intimate connection which this sacrament has with the whole process of Christian initiation' was to be more clearly set forth. Pastoral circumstances in some countries, including those of western Europe, have led in the past to the situation in which children have been admitted to First Communion and only confirmed some years later. It is now insisted at innumerable points in the new orders of service and their introductory material that initiation is a process or a journey (*iter*) which sacramentally speaking begins with baptism, is carried a stage forward in confirmation, and is completed in Holy Communion. To transpose the order of confirmation and First Communion is thus a perversion of the tradition of the western Church which as we have seen is first attested by Tertullian and the *Apostolic Tradition.* But whether this tradition is as secure and as universal, even in the records of the western Church, as could be wished, and whether it is based on a sound foundation of theological and biblical study, is perhaps not entirely clear.

Confirmation may be administered either within the Mass or otherwise. In either case the service begins with a Celebration of God's Word. Then, when the candidates have been presented, a homily is read to them at the end of which they are invited to renew the promises which either they or their parents and godparents made at their baptism. In fact, as we have already noted, the new order for the baptism of children requires that parents and godparents make promises on their own behalf but not on behalf of their children. The introduction of the renewal of baptismal vows into the confirmation service dates from an Instruction of the Sacred Congregation of Rites in 1964. The renewal of baptismal vows by the faithful present at the Easter vigil was first introduced into the Holy Week rites in 1956. The new rites include other reminders of baptism. Thus even if there is no one to be baptized at the vigil service (though increasingly there is), water is nevertheless to be blessed in a special prayer and the priest sprinkles the people with it to remind them of their baptism. Similarly the sprinkling of water at the *Asperges* before Mass is now presented as a reminder of baptism.

While the bishop says the prayer for the sevenfold gifts of the Spirit, any other priests who are associated with him may also extend their hands over the candidates, and in the performance of the sacrament itself, if the number of candidates requires it, the bishop may delegate to the priests a share in the administration of the sacrament. He may also delegate the administration of the sacrament to priests in his absence.

THE RITE OF CHRISTIAN INITIATION OF ADULTS 1972

In this section of the initiation rites, the third to be published, the catechumenate is restored in several distinct steps, as the Constitution on the Sacred Liturgy requires. The *Gelasian Sacramentary* (DBL, pp. 166ff) preserves no more than the skeleton of the rites of the catechumenate in preparation for baptism, because it dates from a period when adult baptism had become a rarity and infant baptism was the normal practice. The new provision follows much the same outline, but its material is as much pastoral as liturgical and clothes the bare bones of liturgical forms with explanatory and pastoral matter. It also allows a great deal of flexibility to take account of varying circumstances, especially those where converts turn to Christ from heathen backgrounds.

The first stage begins with the rite by which converts are admitted to be catechumens. This is a public rite and may take place either in church or elsewhere. The converts affirm their desire for eternal life. In places where 'false worship flourishes' there may be an exorcism, an insufflation, and a renunciation; the giving of salt and other symbolic acts are not excluded. The celebrant then signs the converts on the forehead, and by this act they become catechumens and may be given a cross in token of their new estate. Catechists and sponsors may also sign them on the organs of sense. The catechumens are then invited into the church, if they are not already there, for the celebration of the word of God, and may be given a copy of the Gospels. Each part of the service is marked by prayer or thanksgiving, and it ends with prayers for the catechumens. If the Eucharist follows they are dismissed but do not immediately disperse: 'with the help of some of the faithful they remain together to share their fraternal joy and spiritual experiences'.

The catechumenate continues 'until they have matured sufficiently' and may last for several years. The period is observed by instruction and attendance at the ministry of the word; by minor exorcisms; by blessings; and by anointing with the oil of catechumens.

The second stage of initiation begins at the beginning of Lent. All who are pastorally concerned with the catechumens decide which are suitable to proceed to baptism, and their enrolment and admission to the ranks of the 'elect' takes place formally and in public after the homily on the First Sunday of Lent. The three scrutinies are performed at Mass on the Third, Fourth, and Fifth Sundays of Lent, on which the gospel is devoted respectively to the Samaritan woman, the man born blind, and the raising of Lazarus (see DBL, p. 133): in these circumstances the lessons for Year A are always to be used. The elect and their sponsors stand out before the celebrant, who invites the sponsors to pray and the elect to bow their heads or kneel. After silent prayer, a litany of prayer is said for the elect. The exorcism follows. The celebrant says a prayer for protection over all the candidates, and then lays his hand on each in silence. Then, extending his hands over them all he prays that God will 'command the spirit of evil to leave them'.

The Presentation of the creed takes place at Mass during the week following the first scrutiny and the Presentation of the Lord's Prayer during the week following the third scrutiny, although it is permitted that these may be done during the catechumenate. Special lessons may replace those of the normal weekday Mass. On these occasions the Apostles' creed (the Nicene creed also, if desired) and the Lord's Prayer are formally recited to the elect and commended to their respect.

On Holy Saturday the elect may be gathered together for a final meeting to dispose them to receive the sacraments of initiation on the following night. This meeting may include a recitation (return) of the creed, the *Effeta,* the giving of a Christian name, and an anointing with the oil of catechumens.

The third stage is the Celebration of the Sacraments of Initiation, which is not essentially different from the forms which we have already examined. Commenting on this whole long performance from the admission to the catechumenate to the final rites of initiation, C. J. Walsh[51] says: 'Many will be tempted to dismiss this entire liturgy as impractical, unnecessary, artificial and excessively complex, something which could only have been devised by academics and romantics quite out of touch with pastoral realities. But they should be reminded that the catechumenate was successfully restored in France as long ago as 1953, and that the leader of the group which produced the new rite has had twenty years' experience of running such catechumenates. Organized catechumenates exist in every diocese in France and are staffed by qualified personnel.' Walsh goes on to claim that what is done in France might just as well be done in England, and ought to be done.

9

Bibliography

It has long been customary in the Church of England to refer to the baptism services as 'occasional offices', and so to reduce them to the same level as the marriage and funeral rites. This disrespectful treatment of the first of the gospel sacraments has a long history, and is well exemplified in the two seventh-century letters expounding the liturgy which were falsely ascribed to St Germanus of Paris. The first of these letters is an exposition of the rites of the Eucharist: in the second (DBL, p. 164) the writer undertook to set out 'various charismata of the Church', and in this all-embracing expression he included his comments on antiphons, ecclesiastical dress, and the *rites of baptism.* Until recently the literature of liturgical study has revealed the same disparity of treatment, with no lack of books about the Eucharist but relatively few about baptism. It is therefore a pleasure to record that the last few decades have produced a useful crop of books and other studies relating to the liturgy of baptism. A complete survey of them would be a major task, and the following notes set out only some of the more important books and studies of the subject to which this present work provides an introduction.

General liturgical manuals

A New History of the Book of Common Prayer, by Procter and Frere, deals mainly with the Reformation and the subsequent history of the Prayer Book. Much the same ground is covered in G. J. Cuming, *A History of Anglican Liturgy* (London 1969). A second edition of this important book, giving some account of the circumstances which led up to the Alternative Service Book, is to be expected before very long. L. Duchesne's

Christian Worship, translated from the fourth French edition, in several English editions up to 1910, is an introduction to the patristic rites but now very out of date, particularly in regarding the rite of St Cyril of Jerusalem as typical of the early eastern rite. More useful is *The Study of Liturgy,* ed. C. Jones, G. Wainwright, E. Yarnold (London 1978). Nearly seventy pages of this book are devoted to a conspectus of the history of the initiation rites from the New Testament to the present day, including the rites of the eastern Orthodox Church and the Reformed Churches. See also A. G. Martimort, *L'Eglise en Prière* (Paris 1965); E. T. *The Church at Prayer,* vol. 2 (Irish Univ. Press).

Books on the Liturgy of Baptism and Confirmation

The standard study in English has been T. Thompson, *The Offices of Baptism and Confirmation* (Cambridge 1914), which is concerned with the period from the apostolic age to *c.*800 both in East and West. Though out of date and out of print, it remains full of useful information, and no other English work provides the same invaluable analysis of the developed rites of the eastern Church. More recently the publications of the Alcuin Club have included a massive contribution to the study of the initiation rites, as follows:

E. C. Whitaker, *Documents of the Baptismal Liturgy* (1960). The second and revised edition of this was published by S.P.C.K. in 1970.

J. D. C. Fisher, *Christian Initiation: Baptism in the Medieval West* (1965). This is a survey of the development of western rites from the fourth century to the Reformation, showing how confirmation came to be detached from baptism and the Eucharist from both.

L. L. Mitchell, *Baptismal Anointing* (1966) examines the anointings which take place at various points in the rites of East and West, and their origins.

J. D. C. Fisher, *Christian Initiation: The Reformation Period* (1970) is a collection of documents both Catholic and reformed, with commentary.

P. J. Jagger, *Christian Initiation 1552-1969* (1970) is a collection of texts of baptism and confirmation services, mostly modern, from the Anglican Communion and other sources. It includes the Roman Catholic rites of 1964 and 1969.

J. D. C. Fisher, *Confirmation Then and Now* (1978) examines confirmation rites of East and West, the pre-baptismal anointing of the early eastern Church, and discusses the present controversy.

Taken together these books provide an invaluable study of the history of the Church's rites of initiation, covering the greater part of it. Two important gaps are the first four centuries and the developed rites of the eastern Churches. Baptism in the New Testament and the apostolic age is mostly discussed in books which belong to the field of New Testament rather than liturgical studies. For a discussion of such matters as infant baptism, Jewish proselyte baptism, our Lord's baptism, and the apostolic practice of baptism we must turn to such books as *The New Testament Doctrine of Baptism,* by W. F. Flemington (London 1948); *Baptism in the New Testament,* by Oscar Cullmann (London 1954); and again *Baptism in the New Testament,* by G. R. Beasley-Murray. A careful examination of the New Testament evidence for baptismal liturgy in the apostolic age is provided by C. F. D. Moule in *Worship in the New Testament.* This very useful work was originally published in 1961 and is now reprinted by Grove Books in Liturgical Studies nos. 12 and 13. The very scanty information which comes to us from Christian writers of the second century has been carefully examined by A. Benoit in *Le Baptême chrétien au second siècle* (Paris 1953). There is no comprehensive study in English of the developed rites of the eastern Church. Latin texts of these elaborate rites have been edited by H. Denzinger

95

in *Ritus Orientalium,* which was originally published in 1863 and reprinted in Graz in 1961.

The Apostolic Tradition of Hippolytus

Hippolytus was a notable and controversial figure in the Roman Church at the end of the second century. It is known that he wrote a work which today we call *The Apostolic Tradition.* The important thing to note about this work is that no complete copy in its original Greek exists today. What we do possess is a number of very much revised texts in a variety of oriental languages and a Latin text which is fragmentary, badly translated, and not always reliable. Attempts to reconstruct the original from these sources have been made by G. Dix in *The Apostolic Tradition of Hippolytus* (second edition with preface and corrections by H. Chadwick, London 1968: English translation with Latin and Greek texts); by B. Botte, *La Tradition Apostolique de Saint Hippolyte* (Munster 1963 and 1972: French translation and composite oriental text in Latin); and by G. J. Cuming in *Hippolytus: A Text for Students* (Grove Liturgical Studies, no. 8: see also essay by E. C. Whitaker in a companion volume, *Essays on Hippolytus* (Grove Liturgical Studies, no. 15). Another massive work relating to *The Apostolic Tradition* is that of J. M. Hanssens, *La Liturgie d'Hippolyte* (vol. 1, Rome 1959, 2nd edition Rome 1965; vol. 2, Rome 1970). Hanssens sought to show that the liturgy attested by Hippolytus was Alexandrian rather than Roman. Most scholars today seem to be moving to the conclusion that this work reflects the liturgical practice of the Roman Church at the beginning of the third century.

Fonts and Baptisteries

A study of fonts and baptisteries in East and West has been written by J. G. Davies in *The Architectural Setting of Baptism* (London 1962), showing that the study of the rites of baptism ought to include an appreciation of the architectural setting in which the rite is performed. His book includes a useful passage on the decorative themes which appear in fonts and baptisteries. Other passages on this important subject are to be found in *Baptism and Christian Archaeology,* by C. F. Rogers, Studia Biblica et Ecclesiastica vol. 5 (1903), pp. 239-362; see also H. Lietzmann, *A History of the Early Church* (London 1937-51), vol. 2, pp. 140ff; and J. Danielou, *The Christian Centuries,* vol. 1, pp. 169ff. The use of Old Testament themes by the Fathers to illuminate Christian baptism is discussed by J. Daniélou in *The Bible and the Liturgy* (London 1956).

The Form of Baptism

The most important study of this in modern times is in the article 'Baptême', by P. de Puniet in the *Dictionnaire d'Archéologie chrétienne et de Liturgie (DACL).* See also articles by the present writer, 'The Baptismal Formula in the Syrian Rite', *Church Quarterly Review* (1960), pp. 346-52; and 'The History of the Baptismal Formula', *Journal of Ecclesiastical History* (1965), pp. 1-12. The study of the Apostles' Creed is closely related to the study of the form of baptism, and J. N. D. Kelly's *Early Christian Creeds* (London 1950) is the definitive study of the origins and development of the creeds. A different approach to the history of the baptismal formula is to be found in *Early Christian Baptism and the Creed,* by J. H. Crehan (London 1950).

Confirmation

A. J. Mason, in *The Relation of Confirmation to Baptism* (London 1893), first propounded the view that baptism and confirmation are separate parts of one sacrament of initiation. This view was supported by G. Dix in *The Theology of Confirmation in relation to Baptism* (London 1946), and more recently by J. D. C. Fisher in a contribution to *Crisis for*

Confirmation, ed. M. Perry (London 1967). A contrary view, supporting the apparent meaning of the Prayer Book and the Thirty Nine Articles, is set out by G. W. H. Lampe in *The Seal of the Spirit* (2nd edition London 1967). A good example of the belief that baptism is the sacrament for innocence and confirmation for maturity is found in Darwell Stone's *Holy Baptism* (London 1912) in the Oxford Library of Practical Theology. All these views are reflected in a crop of convocation and synod reports and other smaller studies. These have been listed and discussed in E. C. Whitaker, *Sacramental Initiation Complete in Baptism,* Grove Liturgical Studies no. 1.

The Early Syrian Rites

Two very important collections of essays are to be found in *L'Orient Syrien,* vol. 1 (Paris 1956), ed. G. Khouri-Sarkis; and *Studies on Syrian Baptismal Rites,* ed. J. Vellian, Syrian Churches Series vol. 6 (Kottayam 1973). Important surveys of the evidence have been made by S. P. Brock, *The Holy Spirit in the Syrian Baptismal Tradition,* Syrian Churches Series vol. 9, and J. D. C. Fisher, *Confirmation Then and Now* (Alcuin Club 1978). Volumes of the Syrian Churches Series may conveniently be obtained from The Fellowship of St Alban and St Sergius. For a reply to some of Brock's arguments, see article by the present writer, 'The Prayer *Pater Sancte* in the Syrian Orthodox Baptismal Liturgy', in *Journal of Theological Studies,* vol. 28, pp. 525-8.

Modern Rites

A large number of modern rites has been assembled in P. J. Jagger, *Christian Initiation 1552-1969* (Alcuin Club 1970), including the Series Two services of confirmation and infant baptism of the Church of England, and some of the Roman Catholic rites of 1964 and 1969. Studies of the services in the Alternative Service Book are as yet only few and written by people involved in their composition. C. O. Buchanan has written a study of these services in *Liturgy for Initiation* (Grove Booklets on Ministry and Worship no. 65), and the *Commentary* by the Liturgical Commission includes an introduction to the initiation services. A study of the Roman Catholic rites of infant baptism and confirmation is included in J. D. Crichton's *Christian Celebration: The Sacraments* (London 1973). J. D. Crichton is by no means uncritical of the rites which he discusses, and his book is immensely valuable to all students of liturgy. Another study of the modern Roman Catholic rite is included in an essay by C. J. Walsh in *Pastoral Liturgy, A Symposium,* ed. H. Winstone (London 1975). Walsh is particularly critical of the new rite of confirmation. Translations of the Constitution on the Sacred Liturgy are to be found in two useful books. In *The Church's Worship,* J. D. Crichton provides a text and commentary; in *Liturgy, Renewal and Adaptation,* edited by Austin Flannery, contributors review the circumstances which led up to the reformation of the liturgy and the process by which it was carried out, and the appendix sets out a number of relevant documents of recent years.

The possibility of a common ecumenical structure for the rites of Christian initiation has been discussed in a report of the Joint Liturgical Group, *Initiation and Eucharist,* ed. N. Clark and R. C. D. Jasper (London 1972).

Miscellaneous

Little has been said in this book about godparents or sponsors, a matter which by common custom has been treated in separation from the liturgy itself. A thorough study of the matter has been made by D. S. Bailey under the title *Sponsors at Baptism and Confirmation* (London 1952). Exorcism and the other apotropaic devices which were used in baptism is another subject which has called for separate study. Very little in fact has been written about it, and the only book which deals fully with the subject is *Der Exorcismus im altchristlichen Taufritual,* Studien zur Geschichte des Altertums vol. 3, by F. J. Dolger. Another small study of matters relating to exorcism is that of R. M. Woolley, *Exorcism and the Healing of the Sick* (London 1932).

Some of the matters arising from the study of baptism in the New Testament have demanded special studies in separate books. Thus Joachim Jeremias has argued in *Infant Baptism in the First Four Centuries* (London 1960) that infants were baptized in the apostolic Church. Kurt Aland in *Did the Early Church Baptize Infants?* (London 1962) has maintained the opposite view and provoked a further reply from Jeremias in *The Origins of Infant Baptism* (London 1964). G. R. Beasley-Murray also devotes a substantial section of his *Baptism in the New Testament* to a study of this matter from the theological rather than the historical point of view, and from the standpoint of a Baptist. Other small but useful studies from the Anglican point of view are to be found in *A Case for Infant Baptism,* by C. O. Buchanan; *Infant Baptism under Cross-Examination,* by C. O. Buchanan and D. Pawson; and *One Baptism Once,* by C. O. Buchanan; Grove Booklets on Ministry and Worship, nos. 20, 24, and 61 respectively.

The pre-Christian background to Christian baptism is discussed in the works of Flemington and Beasley-Murray to which we have already referred, and also in a special study of the subject by F. Gavin under the title *The Jewish Antecedents of the Christian Sacraments* (London 1928).

Post-script

A useful background to the early Syrian rite is provided by A. Vööbus in *History of the Syrian Orient,* vols. 1 & 2 (Corpus Scriptorum Christianorum Orientalium: Subsidia, nos. 14 & 17).

S. P. Brock has contributed an essay on 'The Transition to a Post-Baptismal Anointing in the Antiochene Rite' in *The Sacrifice of Praise,* ed. Bryan D. Spinks (Centro Liturgico Vincenziano — Edizioni Liturgiche, Rome, 1980).

The origins of the renewal of baptismal promises in the Roman Catholic rites are traced by J. Rotelle, O.S.A. in an article, 'The Commemoration of Baptism in the Life of a Christian', in *Ephemerides Liturgicae* vol. 86 (1972), pp. 474-85.

Notes

Chapter 1
The Foundations of the Liturgy

1 J. Ysebaert, *Greek Baptismal Terminology* (Nijmegen 1962), pp. 12ff.

2 *An Introduction to the Theology of the New Testament* (London 1958), p. 347.

3 G. R. Beasley-Murray, *Baptism in the New Testament* (London 1962), pp. 18ff.

4 *Documents of the Baptismal Liturgy,* ed. E. C. Whitaker, pp. 49, 55. (This work is cited in the present text as DBL, and references are to the 2nd edition 1970.)

5 J.G.Davies, *The Architectural Setting of Baptism* (London 1962), pp. 25f.

6 See J.D.C. Fisher, 'The Consecration of Water in the Early Rites of Baptism', *Studia Patristica,* vol. 2 (1957), pp. 41-46.

7 Migne, *PL* 35. 1840.

8 M.R. James, ed., *The Apocryphal New Testament* (O.U.P. 1924), p. 279.

9 For Theodore of Mopsuestia, see E.J. Yarnold, *The Awe-Inspiring Rites of Initiation* (London 1971), p. 199.

10 See E.C. Whitaker, 'The History of the Baptismal Formula', *Journal of Ecclesiastical History,* vol. 16 (1961), pp. 1-12.

11 For this paragraph, see J.D.C. Fisher, *Christian Initiation: Baptism in the Medieval West* (Alcuin Club 1965), pp. 120-40.

12 See J.D.C. Fisher, *Christian Initiation: The Reformation Period* (Alcuin Club 1970), p. 258.

13 See J.D.C. Fisher, *Baptism in the Medieval West,* p. 183.

14 For this and the following paragraphs, see chapter on bibliography.

15 As they were by, e.g., Calvin (J.D.C. Fisher, *Christian Initiation: The Reformation Period,* p. 257); G. Dix (*Confirmation, or The*

Laying on of Hands (SPCK 1936), pp. 18ff); A.E.J. Rawlinson *(Christian Initiation* (SPCK 1947), p. 19f); G. Lampe *(The Seal of the Spirit* (London 1951), pp. 69ff).

16 See T. W. Manson, 'Miscellanea Apocalyptica iii', *J.T.S.,* vol. 48: also J. D. C. Fisher, *Confirmation Then and Now,* p. 120.

17 See bibliography, The Early Syrian Rite, for the whole of this paragraph.

18 'Postbaptismal Anointing in the Ancient Patriarchate of Antioch', *Studies on Syrian Baptismal Rites,* pp. 63-71 (Syrian Churches Series, vol. 6 (Kottayam 1973), ed. J. Vellian).

19 E. J. Yarnold, 'The ceremonies of initiation in the *De Sacramentis* and *De Mysteriis* of St Ambrose', *Studia Patristica,* vol. x, pp. 457f.

Chapter 2
Basic Patterns and their Development

20 See quotation from unpublished ms. in A. Wenger, *Huit Catecheses baptismales,* Sources chrétiennes, vol. 50, pp. 100f.

21 See article cited above, note 18.

22 *The Offices of Baptism and Confirmation* (1914), pp. 66f.

23 Denzinger, *Ritus Orientalium,* pp. 364f.

24 'The Old Syrian Baptismal Tradition', *Studies in Church History,* ed. G.J. Cuming, vol. 2, p. 32.

25 *Confirmation Then and Now,* p. 82.

26 G. Dix, *The Shape of the Liturgy,* p. 350.

27 G.J. Cuming, 'Egyptian Elements in the Jerusalem Liturgy', *J.T.S.* n.s. vol. 25 (1974), pp. 117-24.

28 For this paragraph, see Botte's article, 'Post-baptismal Anointing in the Ancient Patriarchate of Antioch', *Studies on Syrian Baptismal Rites* (Syrian Churches Series, vol. 6), pp. 63-71.

29 *PG* 14. 1038C.

30 *PG* 12. 603C.

31 *H.E.* vii. 9.

32 The date of the Canons is now known to be 336-40; see R.G. Coquin, *Canones Hippolyti* (Paris 1966), Patrologia Orientalis 31.2.

33 See article by G.J. Cuming, 'Thmuis revisited: another look at the prayers of bishop Sarapion', *Theological Studies,* vol. 41, no. 3 (Sept. 1980), pp. 568-75.

34 Denzinger, op. cit., p. 273.

35   Denzinger, op. cit., p. 232.

Chapter 4
Adult Baptism in the Western Church

36   I.e. Constantine and his mother Helen.

37   Bishop of Ravenna, *c.* 400-50.

38   Missionary bishop in the Balkans from *c.* 370.

Chapter 7
The Initiation Services of the
Alternative Service Book

39   W. H. Frere, *Some Principles of Liturgical Reform* (London 1911), pp. 199ff.

40   For this see C. O. Buchanan, *Liturgy for Initiation,* Grove Booklet on Ministry and Worship no. 65.

41   For a full study of this, see J. D. C. Fisher, *Christian Initiation: Baptism in the Medieval West,* pp. 149-57.

42   See D. R. Dendy, *The Use of Lights in Christian Worship* (Alcuin Club 1959), pp. 120ff.

43   See J. D. C. Fisher, *Confirmation Then and Now,* pp. 150f; also the Ely Report, *Christian Initiation, Birth and Growth in the Christian Society,* pp. 33, 35f.

44   J. D. C. Fisher, *Christian Initiation: The Reformation Period,* pp. 218f.

45   J. D. Crichton, *Christian Celebration: The Sacraments* (London 1973), p. 22.

Chapter 8
The Roman Catholic Initiation Rites
1969-1972

46   For a text of this see bibliography, Modern Rites.

47   See P. J. Jagger, *Christian Initiation 1552-1969,* p. 228.

48   J. D. Crichton, *Christian Celebration: The Sacraments,* p. 22.

49   J. D. Crichton, op. cit., pp. 81, 84.

50   J. D. Crichton, op. cit., p. 103f; C. J. Walsh in *Pastoral Liturgy,* ed. H. Winstone, p. 182.

51   Op. cit., p. 167.

Index

Index

Facing east/west p20 (see Thurian p82)